CAMBRIDGE
UNIVERSITY PRESS

Physics

for Cambridge IGCSE™

EXAM PREPARATION AND PRACTICE

Amanda George and Kavita Sanghvi

Contents

Practical past paper practice

An additional Practical guidance chapter and some digital questions can be found online at Cambridge GO. For more information on how to access and use your digital resource, please see inside front cover.

> How to use this series

This suite of resources supports students and teachers following the Cambridge IGCSE Physics syllabus (0625). All of the components in the series are designed to work together and help students develop the necessary knowledge and skills for this subject. With clear language and style, they are designed for international students.

The coursebook provides coverage of the full Cambridge IGCSE™ Physics syllabus (0625). Each chapter explains facts and concepts, and uses relevant real-world examples of scientific principles to bring the subject to life. Together with a focus on practical work and plenty of active learning opportunities, the coursebook prepares learners for all aspects of their scientific study. Questions and exam-style questions in every chapter help learners to consolidate their understanding and provide practice opportunities to apply their learning.

The teacher's resource contains detailed guidance for all topics of the syllabus, including common misconceptions identifying areas where learners might need extra support, as well as an engaging bank of lesson ideas for each syllabus topic. Differentiation is emphasised with suggestions of appropriate interventions to support and stretch learners. It also contains support for preparing and carrying out all the investigations in the practical workbook, including a set of sample results for when practicals aren't possible. Also included are scaffolded worksheets and unit tests for each chapter, as well as answers to all questions in every resource across this series.

This workbook provides learners with additional opportunities for hands-on practical work, giving them full guidance and support that will help them to develop their investigative skills. These skills include planning investigations, selecting and handling apparatus, creating hypotheses, recording and displaying results, and analysing and evaluating data.

The skills-focused workbook has been constructed to help learners develop the skills that they need as they progress through their Cambridge IGCSE™ Physics course, providing practice of all the topics in the coursebook. A three-tier, scaffolded approach to skills development enables students to progress through 'focus', 'practice' and 'challenge' exercises, ensuring that every learner is supported.

Our research shows that English language skills are the single biggest barrier to students accessing international science. This write-in workbook contains exercises set within the context of IGCSE™ Physics topics to consolidate understanding and embed practice in aspects of language central to the subject.

Mathematics is an integral part of scientific study, and one that learners often find a barrier to progression in science. The Maths Skills for Cambridge IGCSE™ Physics write-in workbook has been written in collaboration with the Association of Science Education, with each chapter focusing on several maths skills that their research concluded that students need to succeed in their Physics course.

The Exam Preparation and Practice resource provides dedicated support for learners in preparing for their final assessments. Hundreds of questions in the book and accompanying digital resource will help learners to check that they understand, and can recall, syllabus concepts. To help learners to show what they know in an exam context, a checklist of exam skills with corresponding questions, and past paper question practice, is also included. Self-assessment and reflection features support learners to identify any areas that need further practice. This resource should be used alongside the coursebook, throughout the course of study, so learners can most effectively increase their confidence and readiness for their exams.

> How to use this book

This book will help you to check that you **know** the content of the syllabus and practise how to **show** this understanding in an exam. It will also help you be cognitively prepared and in the **flow**, ready for your exam. Research has shown that it is important that you do all three of these things, so we have designed the Know, Show, Flow approach to help you prepare effectively for exams.

| Know | You will need to consolidate and then recall a lot of syllabus content. |

| Show | You should demonstrate your knowledge in the context of a Cambridge exam. |

| Flow | You should be cognitively engaged and ready to learn. This means reducing test anxiety. |

Exam skills checklist

Category	Exam skill
Understanding the question	Recognise different question types
	Understand command words
	Mark scheme awareness
Providing an appropriate response	Understand connections between concepts
	Keep to time
	Know what a good answer looks like
Developing supportive behaviours	Reflect on progress
	Manage test anxiety

This **Exam skills checklist** helps you to develop the awareness, behaviours and habits that will support you when revising and preparing for your exams. For more exam skills advice, including understanding command words and managing your time effectively, please go to the **Exam skills chapter**.

Know

The full syllabus content of your IGCSE Physics course is covered in your Cambridge coursebook. This book will provide you with different types of questions to support you as you prepare for your exams. You will answer **Knowledge recall questions** that are designed to make sure you understand a topic, and **Recall and connect questions** to help you recall past learning and connect different concepts.

KNOWLEDGE FOCUS

Knowledge Focus boxes summarise the topics that you will answer questions on in each chapter of this book. You can refer back to your Cambridge coursebook to remind yourself of the full detail of the syllabus content.

You will find **Knowledge recall questions** to make sure you understand a topic, and **Recall and connect questions** to help you recall past learning and connect different concepts. It is recommended that you answer the Knowledge recall questions just after you have covered the relevant topic in class, and then return to them at a later point to check you have properly understood the content.

Knowledge recall question

Testing yourself is a good way to check that your understanding is secure. These questions will help you to recall the core knowledge you have acquired during your course, and highlight any areas where you may need more practice. They are indicated with a blue bar with a gap, at the side of the page. We recommend that you answer the Knowledge recall questions just after you have covered the relevant topic in class, and then return to them at a later point to check you have properly understood the content.

≪ RECALL AND CONNECT ≪

To consolidate your learning, you need to test your memory frequently. These questions will test that you remember what you learned in previous chapters, in addition to what you are practising in the current chapter.

UNDERSTAND THESE TERMS

These list the important vocabulary that you should understand for each chapter. Definitions are provided in the glossary of your Cambridge coursebook.

Show

Exam questions test specific knowledge, skills and understanding. You need to be prepared so that you have the best opportunity to show what you know in the time you have during the exam. In addition to practising recall of the syllabus content, it is important to build your exam skills throughout the year.

EXAM SKILLS FOCUS

This feature outlines the exam skills you will practise in each chapter, alongside the Knowledge focus. They are drawn from the core set of eight exam skills, listed in the exam skills checklist. You will practise specific exam skills, such as understanding command words, within each chapter. More general exam skills, such as managing text anxiety, are covered in the Exam skills chapter.

Exam skills question

These questions will help you to develop your exam skills and demonstrate your understanding. To help you become familiar with exam-style questioning, many of these questions follow the style and use the language of real exam questions, and have allocated marks. They are indicated with a solid red bar at the side of the page.

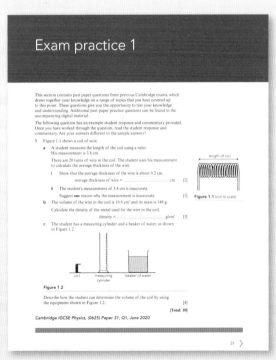

Looking at sample answers to past paper questions helps you to understand what to aim for.

The **Exam practice** sections in this resource contain example student responses and examiner-style commentary showing how the answer could be improved (both written by the authors).

Supplement content

Where content is intended for students who are studying the Supplement content of the syllabus as well as the Core, this is indicated using the arrow and the bar, as on the left here. Supplement questions in the accompanying digital material are flagged in the question titles.

Flow

Preparing for exams can be stressful. One of the approaches recommended by educational psychologists to help with this stress is to improve behaviours around exam preparation. This involves testing yourself in manageable chunks, accompanied by self-evaluation. You should avoid cramming and build in more preparation time. This book is structured to help you do this.

Increasing your ability to recognise the signs of exam-related stress and working through some techniques for how to cope with it will help to make your exam preparation manageable.

REFLECTION

This feature asks you to think about the approach that you take to your exam preparation, and how you might improve this in the future. Reflecting on how you plan, monitor and evaluate your revision and preparation will help you to do your best in your exams.

SELF-ASSESSMENT CHECKLIST

These checklists return to the Learning intentions from your coursebook, as well as the Exam skills focus boxes from each chapter. Checking in on how confident you feel in each of these areas will help you to focus your exam preparation. The 'Show it' prompts will allow you to test your rating. You should revisit any areas that you rate 'Needs more work' or 'Almost there'.

Knowledge and Exam focus	Show it	Needs more work	Almost there	Confident to move on

Increasing your ability to recognise the signs of exam-related stress and working through some techniques for how to cope with it will help to make your exam preparation manageable. The **Exam skills chapter** will support you with this.

Digital support

Extra self-assessment questions for all chapters can be found online at Cambridge GO. For more information on how to access and use your digital resource, please see inside the front cover.

You will find **Answers** for all of the questions in the book on the 'supporting resources' area of the Cambridge GO platform.

Multiple choice questions

These ask you to select the correct answer to a question from four options. These are auto-marked and feedback is provided.

Flip card questions

These present a question on one screen, and suggested answers on the reverse.

Syllabus assessment objectives for IGCSE Physics

You should be familiar with the Assessment Objectives from the syllabus, as the examiner will be looking for evidence of these requirements in your responses and allocating marks accordingly.

The assessment objectives for this syllabus are:

Assessment objective	IGCSE weighting
AO1: Knowledge and Understanding	50%
AO2: Application	30%
AO3: Analysis	20%

Exam skills

by Lucy Parsons

What's the point of this book?

Most students make one really basic mistake when they're preparing for exams. What is it? It's focusing far too much on learning 'stuff' – that's facts, figures, ideas, information – and not nearly enough time practising exam skills.

The students who work really, really hard but are disappointed with their results are nearly always students who focus on memorising stuff. They think to themselves, 'I'll do practice papers once I've revised everything.' The trouble is, they start doing practice papers too late to really develop and improve how they communicate what they know.

What could they do differently?

When your final exam script is assessed, it should contain specific language, information and thinking skills in your answers. If you read a question in an exam and you have no idea what you need to do to give a good answer, the likelihood is that your answer won't be as brilliant as it could be. That means your grade won't reflect the hard work you've put into revising for the exam.

There are different types of questions used in exams to assess different skills. You need to know how to recognise these question types and understand what you need to show in your answers.

So, how do you understand what to do in each question type?

That's what this book is all about. But first a little background.

Meet Benjamin Bloom

The psychologist Benjamin Bloom developed a way of classifying and valuing different skills we use when we learn, such as analysis and recalling information. We call these thinking skills. It's known as Bloom's Taxonomy and it's what most exam questions are based around.

If you understand Bloom's Taxonomy, you can understand what any type of question requires you to do. So, what does it look like?

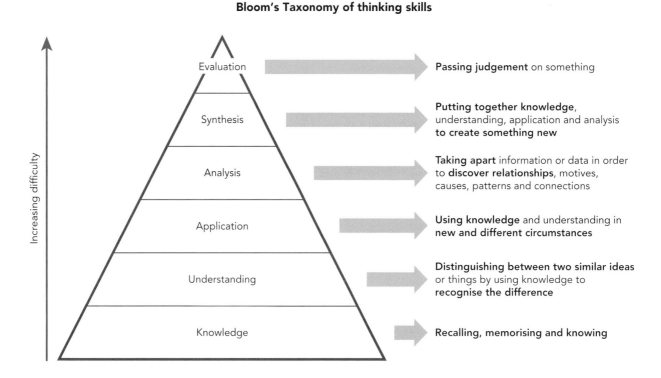

The key things to take away from this diagram are:

- Knowledge and understanding are known as lower-level thinking skills. They are less difficult than the other thinking skills. Exam questions that just test you on what you know are usually worth the lowest number of marks.

- All the other thinking skills are worth higher numbers of marks in exam questions. These questions need you to have some foundational knowledge and understanding but are far more about how you think than what you know. They involve:

  - Taking what you know and using it in unfamiliar situations (application).

  - Going deeper into information to discover relationships, motives, causes, patterns and connections (analysis).

  - Using what you know and think to create something new – whether that's an essay, long-answer exam question a solution to a maths problem, or a piece of art (synthesis).

  - Assessing the value of something, e.g. the reliability of the results of a scientific experiment (evaluation).

In this introductory chapter, you'll be shown how to develop the skills that enable you to communicate what you know and how you think. This will help you achieve to the best of your abilities. In the rest of the book, you'll have a chance to practise these exam skills by understanding how questions work and understanding what you need to show in your answers.

Every time you pick up this book and do a few questions, you're getting closer to achieving your dream results. So, let's get started!

Exam preparation and revision skills

What is revision?

If you think about it, the word 'revision' has two parts to it:

*   re – which means 'again'

*   vision – which is about seeing.

So, revision is literally about 'seeing again'. This means you're looking at something that you've already learned.

Typically, a teacher will teach you something in class. You may then do some questions on it, write about it in some way, or even do a presentation. You might then have an end-of-topic test sometime later. To prepare for this test, you need to 'look again' or revise what you were originally taught.

Step 1: Making knowledge stick

Every time you come back to something you've learned or revised you're improving your understanding and memory of that particular piece of knowledge. This is called **spaced retrieval**. This is how human memory works. If you don't use a piece of knowledge by recalling it, you lose it.

Everything we learn has to be physically stored in our brains by creating neural connections – joining brain cells together. The more often we 'retrieve' or recall a particular piece of knowledge, the stronger the neural connection gets. It's like lifting weights – the more often you lift, the stronger you get.

However, if you don't use a piece of knowledge for a long time, your brain wants to recycle the brain cells and use them for another purpose. The neural connections get weaker until they finally break, and the memory has gone. This is why it's really important to return often to things that you've learned in the past.

Great ways of doing this in your revision include:

*   Testing yourself using flip cards – use the ones available in the digital resources for this book.

*   Testing yourself (or getting someone else to test you) using questions you've created about the topic.

*   Checking your recall of previous topics by answering the Recall and connect questions in this book.

*   Blurting – writing everything you can remember about a topic on a piece of paper in one colour. Then, checking what you missed out and filling it in with another colour. You can do this over and over again until you feel confident that you remember everything.

*   Answering practice questions – use the ones in this book.

*   Getting a good night's sleep to help consolidate your learning.

> **The importance of sleep and creating long-term memory**
>
> When you go to sleep at night, your brain goes through an important process of taking information from your short-term memory and storing it in your long-term memory.
>
> This means that getting a good night's sleep is a very important part of revision. If you don't get enough good quality sleep, you'll actually be making your revision much, much harder.

Step 2: Developing your exam skills

We've already talked about the importance of exam skills, and how many students neglect them because they're worried about covering all the knowledge.

What actually works best is developing your exam skills at the same time as learning the knowledge.

What does this look like in your studies?

- Learning something at school and your teacher setting you questions from this book or from past papers. This tests your recall as well as developing your exam skills.

- Choosing a topic to revise, learning the content and then choosing some questions from this book to test yourself at the same time as developing your exam skills.

The reason why practising your exam skills is so important is that it helps you to get good at communicating what you know and what you think. The more often you do that, the more fluent you'll become in showing what you know in your answers.

Step 3: Getting feedback

The final step is to get feedback on your work.

If you're testing yourself, the feedback is what you got wrong or what you forgot. This means you then need to go back to those things to remind yourself or improve your understanding. Then, you can test yourself again and get more feedback. You can also congratulate yourself for the things you got right – it's important to celebrate any success, big or small.

If you're doing past paper questions or the practice questions in this book, you will need to mark your work. Marking your work is one of the most important things you can do to improve. It's possible to make significant improvements in your marks in a very short space of time when you start marking your work.

Why is marking your own work so powerful? It's because it teaches you to identify the strengths and weaknesses of your own work. When you look at the mark scheme and see how it's structured, you will understand what is needed in your answers to get the results you want.

This doesn't just apply to the knowledge you demonstrate in your answers. It also applies to the language you use and whether it's appropriately subject-specific, the structure of your answer, how you present it on the page and many other factors. Understanding, practising and improving on these things are transformative for your results.

The most important thing about revision

The most important way to make your revision successful is to make it active.

Sometimes, students say they're revising when they sit staring at their textbook or notes for hours at a time. However, this is a really ineffective way to revise because it's passive. In order to make knowledge and skills stick, you need to be doing something like the suggestions in the following diagram. That's why testing yourself and pushing yourself to answer questions that test higher-level thinking skills are so effective. At times, you might actually be able to feel the physical changes happening in your brain as you develop this new knowledge and these new skills. That doesn't come about without effort.

The important thing to remember is that while active revision feels much more like hard work than passive revision, you don't actually need to do nearly as much of it. That's because you remember knowledge and skills when you use active revision. When you use passive revision, it is much, much harder for the knowledge and skills to stick in your memory.

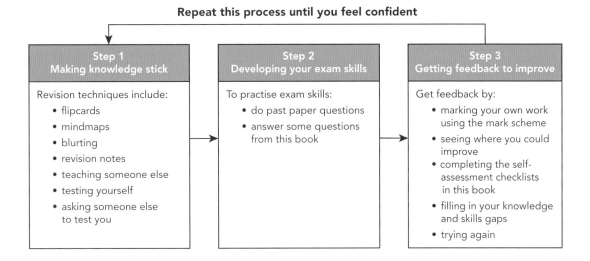

How to improve your exam skills

This book helps you to improve in eight different areas of exam skills, which are divided across three categories. These skills are highlighted in this book in the Exam skills focus at the start of each chapter and developed throughout the book using targeted questions, advice and reflections.

1   **Understand the questions: what are you being asked to do?**

- Know your question types.

- Understand command words.

- Work with mark scheme awareness.

2   **How to answer questions brilliantly**

- Understand connections between concepts.

- Keep to time.

- Know what a good answer looks like.

3   **Give yourself the best chance of success**

- Reflection on progress.

- How to manage test anxiety.

Understand the questions: what are you being asked to do?

Know your question types

In any exam, there will be a range of different question types. These different question types will test different types of thinking skills from Bloom's Taxonomy.

It is very important that you learn to recognise different question types. If you do lots of past papers, over time you will begin to recognise the structure of the paper for each of your subjects. You will know which types of questions may come first and which ones are more likely to come at the end of the paper. You can also complete past paper questions in the Exam practice sections in this book for additional practice.

You will also recognise the differences between questions worth a lower number of marks and questions worth more marks. The key differences are:

- how much you will need to write in your answer
- how sophisticated your answer needs to be in terms of the detail you give and the depth of thinking you show.

Types of questions

1 **Multiple-choice questions**

Multiple-choice questions are generally worth smaller numbers of marks. You will be given several possible answers to the question, and you will have to work out which one is correct using your knowledge and skills.

There is a chance of you getting the right answer with multiple-choice questions even if you don't know the answer. This is why you must **always give an answer for multiple-choice questions** as it means there is a chance you will earn the mark.

Multiple-choice questions are often harder than they appear. The possible answers can be very similar to each other. This means you must be confident in how you work out answers or have a high level of understanding to tell the difference between the possible answers.

Being confident in your subject knowledge and doing lots of practice multiple-choice questions will set you up for success. Use the resources in this book and the accompanying online resources to build your confidence.

This example of a multiple-choice question is worth one mark. You can see that all the answers have one part in common with at least one other answer. For example, palisade cells is included in three of the possible answers. That's why you have to really know the detail of your content knowledge to do well with multiple-choice questions.

Which two types of cells are found in plant leaves?

    A   Palisade mesophyll and stomata

    B   Palisade mesophyll and root hair

    C   Stomata and chloroplast

    D   Chloroplast and palisade mesophyll

2 Questions requiring longer-form answers

Questions requiring longer-form answers need you to write out your answer yourself.

With these questions, take careful note of how many marks are available and how much space you've been given for your answer. These two things will give you a good idea about how much you should say and how much time you should spend on the question.

A rough rule to follow is to write one sentence, or make one point, for each mark that is available. You will get better and better at these longer form questions the more you practise them.

In this example of a history question, you can see it is worth four marks. It is not asking for an explanation, just for you to list Lloyd George's aims. Therefore, you need to make four correct points in order to get full marks.

What were Lloyd George's aims during negotiations leading to the Treaty of Versailles?   [4]

3 Essay questions

Essay questions are the longest questions you will be asked to answer in an exam. They examine the higher-order thinking skills from Bloom's Taxonomy such as analysis, synthesis and evaluation.

To do well in essay questions, you need to talk about what you know, giving your opinion, comparing one concept or example to another, and evaluating your own ideas or the ones you're discussing in your answer.

You also need to have a strong structure and logical argument that guides the reader through your thought process. This usually means having an introduction, some main body paragraphs that discuss one point at a time, and a conclusion.

Essay questions are usually level-marked. This means that you don't get one mark per point you make. Instead, you're given marks for the quality of the ideas you're sharing as well as how well you present those ideas through the subject-specific language you use and the structure of your essay.

Practising essays and becoming familiar with the mark scheme is the only way to get really good at them.

Understand command words

What are command words?

Command words are the most important words in every exam question. This is because command words tell you what you need to do in your answer. Do you remember Bloom's Taxonomy? Command words tell you which thinking skill you need to demonstrate in the answer to each question.

Two very common command words are **describe** and **explain**.

When you see the command word describe in a question, you're being asked to show lower-order thinking skills like knowledge and understanding. The question will either be worth fewer marks, or you will need to make more points if it is worth more marks.

The command word explain is asking you to show higher-order thinking skills. When you see the command word explain, you need to be able to say how or why something happens.

You need to understand all of the relevant command words for the subjects you are taking. Ask your teacher where to find them if you are not sure. It's best not to try to memorise the list of command words, but to become familiar with what command words are asking for by doing lots of practice questions and marking your own work.

How to work with command words

When you first see an exam question, read it through once. Then, read it through again and identify the command word(s). Underline the command word(s) to make it clear to yourself which they are every time you refer back to the question.

You may also want to identify the **content** words in the question and underline them with a different colour. Content words tell you which area of knowledge you need to draw on to answer the question.

In this example, command words are shown in red and content words in blue:

1   a   Explain **four** reasons why governments might support business start-ups.   [8]

> *Adapted from Cambridge IGCSE Business Studies (0450)*
> *Q1a Paper 21 June 2022*

Marking your own work using the mark scheme will help you get even better at understanding command words and knowing how to give good answers for each.

Work with mark scheme awareness

The most transformative thing that any student can do to improve their marks is to work with mark schemes. This means using mark schemes to mark your own work at every opportunity.

Many students are very nervous about marking their own work as they do not feel experienced or qualified enough. However, being brave enough to try to mark your own work and taking the time to get good at it will improve your marks hugely.

Why marking your own work makes such a big difference

Marking your own work can help you to improve your answers in the following ways:

1   Answering the question

Having a deep and detailed understanding of what is required by the question enables you to answer the question more clearly and more accurately.

It can also help you to give the required information using fewer words and in less time, as you can avoid including unrelated points or topics in your answer.

2   Using subject-specific vocabulary

Every subject has subject-specific vocabulary. This includes technical terms for objects or concepts in a subject, such as mitosis and meiosis in biology. It also includes how you talk about the subject, using appropriate vocabulary that may differ from everyday language. For example, in any science subject you might be asked to describe the trend on a graph.

Your answer could say it 'goes up fast' or your answer could say it 'increases rapidly'. You would not get marks for saying 'it goes up fast', but you would for saying it 'increases rapidly'. This is the difference between everyday language and formal, scientific language.

When you answer lots of practice questions, you become fluent in the language specific to your subject.

3 Knowing how much to write

It's very common for students to either write too much or too little to answer questions. Becoming familiar with the mark schemes for many different questions will help you to gain a better understanding of how much you need to write in order to get a good mark.

4 Structuring your answer

There are often clues in questions about how to structure your answer. However, mark schemes give you an even stronger idea of the structure you should use in your answers.

For example, if a question says:

'Describe and explain two reasons why…'

You can give a clear answer by:

- Describing reason 1
- Explaining reason 1
- Describing reason 2
- Explaining reason 2

Having a very clear structure will also make it easier to identify where you have earned marks. This means that you're more likely to be awarded the number of marks you deserve.

5 Keeping to time

Answering the question, using subject-specific vocabulary, knowing how much to write and giving a clear structure to your answer will all help you to keep to time in an exam. You will not waste time by writing too much for any answer. Therefore, you will have sufficient time to give a good answer to every question.

How to answer exam questions brilliantly

Understand connections between concepts

One of the higher-level thinking skills in Bloom's Taxonomy is **synthesis**. Synthesis means making connections between different areas of knowledge. You may have heard about synoptic links. Making synoptic links is the same as showing the thinking skill of synthesis.

Exam questions that ask you to show your synthesis skills are usually worth the highest number of marks on an exam paper. To write good answers to these questions, you need to spend time thinking about the links between the topics you've studied **before** you arrive in your exam. A great way of doing this is using mind maps.

How to create a mind map

To create a mind map:

1   Use a large piece of paper and several different coloured pens.

2   Write the name of your subject in the middle. Then, write the key topic areas evenly spaced around the edge, each with a different colour.

3   Then, around each topic area, start to write the detail of what you can remember. If you find something that is connected with something you studied in another topic, you can draw a line linking the two things together.

This is a good way of practising your retrieval of information as well as linking topics together.

Answering synoptic exam questions

You will recognise questions that require you to make links between concepts because they have a higher number of marks. You will have practised them using this book and the accompanying resources.

To answer a synoptic exam question:

1   **Identify the command and content words.** You are more likely to find command words like **discuss** and **explain** in these questions. They might also have phrases like 'the connection between'.

2   **Make a plan for your answer.** It is worth taking a short amount of time to think about what you're going to write in your answer. Think carefully about what information you're going to put in, the links between the different pieces of information and how you're going to structure your answer to make your ideas clear.

3   **Use linking words and phrases in your answer.** For example, 'therefore', 'because', due to', 'since' or 'this means that'.

Here is an example of an English Literature exam question that requires you to make synoptic links in your answer.

1   Discuss Carol Ann Duffy's exploration of childhood in her poetry.
    Refer to two poems in your answer.   [25]

Content words are shown in blue; command words are shown in red.

This question is asking you to explore the theme of childhood in Duffy's poetry. You need to choose two of her poems to refer to in your answer. This means you need a good knowledge of her poetry, and to be familiar with her exploration of childhood, so that you can easily select two poems that will give you plenty to say in your answer.

Keep to time

Managing your time in exams is really important. Some students do not achieve to the best of their abilities because they run out of time to answer all the questions. However, if you manage your time well, you will be able to attempt every question on the exam paper.

Why is it important to attempt all the questions on an exam paper?

If you attempt every question on a paper, you have the best chance of achieving the highest mark you are capable of.

Students who manage their time poorly in exams will often spend far too long on some questions and not even attempt others. Most students are unlikely to get full marks on many questions, but you will get zero marks for the questions you don't answer. You can maximise your marks by giving an answer to every question.

Minutes per mark

The most important way to keep to time is knowing how many minutes you can spend on each mark.

For example, if your exam paper has 90 marks available and you have 90 minutes, you know there is 1 mark per minute.

Therefore, if you have a 5 mark question, you should spend five minutes on it.

Sometimes, you can give a good answer in less time than you have budgeted using the minutes per mark technique. If this happens, you will have more time to spend on questions that use higher-order thinking skills, or more time on checking your work.

How to get faster at answering exam questions

The best way to get faster at answering exam questions is to do lots of practice. You should practise each question type that will be in your exam, marking your own work, so that you know precisely how that question works and what is required by the question. Use the questions in this book to get better and better at answering each question type.

Use the 'Slow, Slow, Quick' technique to get faster.

Take your time answering questions when you first start practising them. You may answer them with the support of the textbook, your notes or the mark scheme. These things will support you with your content knowledge, the language you use in your answer and the structure of your answer.

Every time you practise this question type, you will get more confident and faster. You will become experienced with this question type, so that it is easy for you to recall the subject knowledge and write it down using the correct language and a good structure.

Calculating marks per minute

Use this calculation to work out how long you have for each mark:

Total time in the exam / Number of marks available = Minutes per mark

Calculate how long you have for a question worth more than one mark like this:

Minutes per mark × Marks available for this question = Number of minutes for this question

What about time to check your work?

It is a very good idea to check your work at the end of an exam. You need to work out if this is feasible with the minutes per mark available to you. If you're always rushing to finish the questions, you shouldn't budget checking time. However, if you usually have time to spare, then you can budget checking time.

To include checking time in your minutes per mark calculation:

(Total time in the exam – Checking time) / Number of marks available = Minutes per mark

Know what a good answer looks like

It is much easier to give a good answer if you know what a good answer looks like.

Use these methods to know what a good answer looks like.

1   **Sample answers** – you can find sample answers in these places:

   • from your teacher

   • written by your friends or other members of your class

   • in this book.

2   **Look at mark schemes** – mark schemes are full of information about what you should include in your answers. Get familiar with mark schemes to gain a better understanding of the type of things a good answer would contain.

3   **Feedback from your teacher** – if you are finding it difficult to improve your exam skills for a particular type of question, ask your teacher for detailed feedback. You should also look at their comments on your work in detail.

Give yourself the best chance of success

Reflection on progress

As you prepare for your exam, it's important to reflect on your progress. Taking time to think about what you're doing well and what could be improved brings more focus to your revision. Reflecting on progress also helps you to continuously improve your knowledge and exam skills.

How do you reflect on progress?

Use the 'reflection' feature in this book to help you reflect on your progress during your exam preparation. Then, at the end of each revision session, take a few minutes to think about the following:

	What went well? What would you do the same next time?	What didn't go well? What would you do differently next time?
Your subject knowledge		
How you revised your subject knowledge – did you use active retrieval techniques?		
Your use of subject-specific and academic language		
Understanding the question by identifying command words and content words		
Giving a clear structure to your answer		
Keeping to time		
Marking your own work		

Remember to check for silly mistakes – things like missing the units out after you carefully calculated your answer.

Use the mark scheme to mark your own work. Every time you mark your own work, you will be recognising the good and bad aspects of your work, so that you can progressively give better answers over time.

When do you need to come back to this topic or skill?

Earlier in this section of the book, we talked about revision skills and the importance of spaced retrieval. When you reflect on your progress, you need to think about how soon you need to return to the topic or skill you've just been focusing on.

For example, if you were really disappointed with your subject knowledge, it would be a good idea to do some more active retrieval and practice questions on this topic tomorrow. However, if you did really well you can feel confident you know this topic and come back to it again in three weeks' or a month's time.

The same goes for exam skills. If you were disappointed with how you answered the question, you should look at some sample answers and try this type of question again soon. However, if you did well, you can move on to other types of exam questions.

Improving your memory of subject knowledge

Sometimes students slip back into using passive revision techniques, such as only reading the coursebook or their notes, rather than also using active revision techniques, like testing themselves using flip cards or blurting.

You can avoid this mistake by observing how well your learning is working as you revise. You should be thinking to yourself, 'Am I remembering this? Am I understanding this? Is this revision working?'

If the answer to any of those questions is 'no', then you need to change what you're doing to revise this particular topic. For example, if you don't understand, you could look up your topic in a different textbook in the school library to see if a different explanation helps. Or you could see if you can find a video online that brings the idea to life.

You are in control

When you're studying for exams it's easy to think that your teachers are in charge. However, you have to remember that you are studying for your exams and the results you get will be yours and no one else's.

That means you have to take responsibility for all your exam preparation. You have the power to change how you're preparing if what you're doing isn't working. You also have control over what you revise and when: you can make sure you focus on your weaker topics and skills to improve your achievement in the subject.

This isn't always easy to do. Sometimes you have to find an inner ability that you have not used before. But, if you are determined enough to do well, you can find what it takes to focus, improve and keep going.

What is test anxiety?

Do you get worried or anxious about exams? Does your worry or anxiety impact how well you do in tests and exams?

Test anxiety is part of your natural stress response.

The stress response evolved in animals and humans many thousands of years ago to help keep them alive. Let's look at an example.

The stress response in the wild

Imagine an impala grazing in the grasslands of east Africa. It's happily and calmly eating grass in its herd in what we would call the parasympathetic state of rest and repair.

Then the impala sees a lion. The impala suddenly panics because its life is in danger. This state of panic is also known as the stressed or sympathetic state. The sympathetic state presents itself in three forms: flight, fight and freeze.

The impala starts to run away from the lion. Running away is known as the flight stress response.

The impala might not be fast enough to run away from the lion. The lion catches it but has a loose grip. The impala struggles to try to get away. This struggle is the fight stress response.

However, the lion gets an even stronger grip on the impala. Now the only chance of the impala surviving is playing dead. The impala goes limp, its heart rate and breathing slows. This is called the freeze stress response. The lion believes that it has killed the impala so it drops the impala to the ground. Now the impala can switch back into the flight response and run away.

The impala is now safe – the different stages of the stress response have saved its life.

What has the impala got to do with your exams?

When you feel test anxiety, you have the same physiological stress responses as an impala being hunted by a lion. Unfortunately, the human nervous system cannot tell the difference between a life-threatening situation, such as being chased by a lion, and the stress of taking an exam.

If you understand how the stress response works in the human nervous system, you will be able to learn techniques to reduce test anxiety.

The role of the vagus nerve in test anxiety

The vagus nerve is the part of your nervous system that determines your stress response. Vagus means 'wandering' in Latin, so the vagus nerve is also known as the 'wandering nerve'. The vagus nerve wanders from your brain, down each side of your body, to nearly all your organs, including your lungs, heart, kidneys, liver, digestive system and bladder.

If you are in a stressful situation, like an exam, your vagus nerve sends a message to all these different organs to activate their stress response. Here are some common examples:

*   **Heart** beats faster.

*   **Kidneys** produce more adrenaline so that you can run, making you fidgety and distracted.

*   **Digestive system** and **bladder** want to eliminate all waste products so that energy can be used for fight or flight.

If you want to feel calmer about your revision and exams, you need to do two things to help you move into the parasympathetic, or rest and repair, state:

1 Work with your vagus nerve to send messages of safety through your body.

2 Change your perception of the test so that you see it as safe and not dangerous.

How to cope with test anxiety

1 Be well prepared

Good preparation is the most important part of managing test anxiety. The better your preparation, the more confident you will be. If you are confident, you will not perceive the test or exam as dangerous, so the sympathetic nervous system responses of fight, flight and freeze are less likely to happen.

This book is all about helping you to be well prepared and building your confidence in your knowledge and ability to answer exam questions well. Working through the knowledge recall questions will help you to become more confident in your knowledge of the subject. The practice questions and exam skills questions will help you to become more confident in communicating your knowledge in an exam.

To be well prepared, look at the advice in the rest of this chapter and use it as you work through the questions in this book.

2 Work with your vagus nerve

The easiest way to work with your vagus nerve to tell it that you're in a safe situation is through your breathing. This means breathing deeply into the bottom of your lungs, so that your stomach expands, and then breathing out for longer than you breathed in. You can do this with counting.

Breathe in deeply, expanding your abdomen, for the count of four; breathe out drawing your navel back towards your spine for the count of five, six or seven. Repeat this at least three times. However, you can do it for as long as it takes for you to feel calm.

The important thing is that you breathe out for longer than you breathe in. This is because when you breathe in, your heart rate increases slightly, and when you breathe out, your heart rate decreases slightly. If you're spending more time breathing out overall, you will be decreasing your heart rate over time.

3 Feel it

Anxiety is an uncomfortable, difficult thing to feel. That means that many people try to run away from anxious feelings. However, this means the stress just gets stored in your body for you to feel later.

When you feel anxious, follow these four steps:

1 Pause.

2 Place one hand on your heart and one hand on your stomach.

3 Notice what you're feeling.

4 Stay with your feelings.

What you will find is that if you are willing to experience what you feel for a minute or two, the feeling of anxiety will usually pass very quickly.

4   **Write or talk it out**

If your thoughts are moving very quickly, it is often better to get them out of your mind and on to paper.

You could take a few minutes to write down everything that comes through your mind, then rip up your paper and throw it away. If you don't like writing, you can speak aloud alone or to someone you trust.

Other ways to break the stress cycle

Exercise and movement	Being friendly	Laughter
• Run or walk. • Dance. • Lift weights. • Yoga. Anything that involves moving your body is helpful.	• Chat to someone in your study break. • Talk to the cashier when you buy your lunch.	• Watch or listen to a funny show on TV or online. • Talk with someone who makes you laugh. • Look at photos of fun times.
Have a hug	**Releasing emotions**	**Creativity**
• Hug a friend or relative. • Cuddle a pet e.g. a cat. Hug for 20 seconds or until you feel calm and relaxed.	It is healthy to release negative or sad emotions. Crying is often a quick way to get rid of these difficult feelings so if you feel like you need to cry, allow it.	• Paint, draw or sketch. • Sew, knit or crochet. • Cook, build something.

If you have long-term symptoms of anxiety, it is important to tell someone you trust and ask for help.

Your perfect revision session

1 Intention

What do you want to achieve in this revision session?
- Choose an area of knowledge or an exam skill that you want to focus on.
- Choose some questions from this book that focus on this knowledge area or skill.
- Gather any other resources you will need e.g. pen, paper, flashcards, coursebook.

2 Focus

Set your focus for the session
- Remove distractions from your study area e.g. leave your phone in another room.
- Write down on a piece of paper or sticky note the knowledge area or skill you're intending to focus on.
- Close your eyes and take three deep breaths, with the exhale longer than the inhale.

3 Revision

Revise your knowledge and understanding
- To improve your knowledge and understanding of the topic, use your coursebook, notes or flashcards, including active learning techniques.
- To improve your exam skills, look at previous answers, teacher feedback, mark schemes, sample answers or examiners' reports.

4 Practice

Answer practice questions
- Use the questions in this book, or in the additional online resources, to practise your exam skills.
- If the exam is soon, do this in timed conditions without the support of the coursebook or your notes.
- If the exam is a long time away, you can use your notes and resources to help you.

5 Feedback

Mark your answers
- Use mark schemes to mark your work.
- Reflect on what you've done well and what you could do to improve next time.

6 Next steps

What have you learned about your progress from this revision session? What do you need to do next?
- What did you do well? Feel good about these things, and know it's safe to set these things aside for a while.
- What do you need to work on? How are you going to improve? Make a plan to get better at the things you didn't do well or didn't know.

7 Rest

Take a break
- Do something completely different to rest: get up, move or do something creative or practical.
- Remember that rest is an important part of studying, as it gives your brain a chance to integrate your learning.

1 Making measurements

1 >

KNOWLEDGE FOCUS

In this chapter, you will answer questions on:

- measuring length and volume
- density
- measuring time.

EXAM SKILLS FOCUS

In this chapter you will:

- show that you understand the command word 'determine' and can answer 'determine' questions.

In order to be confident when approaching an exam, it's necessary to be aware of exam skills required and to practise them regularly. Each chapter will help you to focus on the skills and knowledge you need to demonstrate and to give you practice in using them.

When you read an exam question, look carefully at the command word used. It's important to understand what each command word means and what it is asking you to do.

In this chapter you will practise answering questions that use the command word 'determine'.

| Determine | establish an answer using the information available. |

The command word 'determine' is often used when you need to use information from a diagram, graph or table. Sometimes it will be necessary to carry out a calculation to find the answer.

1.1 Measuring length and volume

1   How many:

    a   millimetres are in a centimetre?

    b   metres are in a kilometre?

    c   decimetres are in a kilometre?

    d   millimetres are in a metre?

2   Name two units of volume that are used in the SI system and write their symbols.

3   Figure 1.1 shows the top of some water in a measuring cylinder that shows volume in cubic centimetres. Three positions for reading the volume are shown.

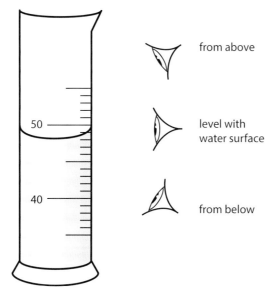

Figure 1.1: Water in a measuring cylinder, with three possible viewing angles

    a   Which position will give the most accurate reading?

    b   What is the volume of the water in the measuring cylinder?

4   A student is planning a craft project. They will use glue that they buy in solid sticks.

They have five identical sticks of solid glue that are cylindrical in shape. They place them side by side between two wooden blocks against a ruler, as shown in Figure 1.2.

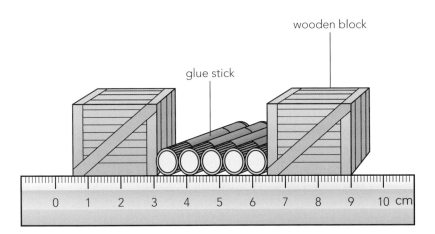

wooden block

glue stick

Figure 1.2

a Determine the diameter of a single glue stick in cm. [2]

b Explain why it is better to find the diameter by measuring several sticks together, instead of measuring just one stick. [1]

c The length of each glue stick is 10 cm. Show that the volume of one glue stick is 3.8 cm^3. [2]

d For their craft project, the student will make star shapes. Each star uses 200 mm^3 of glue. Calculate the number of stars the student can make using one whole glue stick. [2]

[Total: 7]

REFLECTION

Have you successfully memorised the definitions of the key terms in the box? How do you know?

You could test yourself by trying to say or write down the definitions without looking at them, and then check whether your definitions were correct. If you don't recall them all correctly, test yourself again every few days until you can.

By doing this you can avoid 'cramming' – trying to memorise a lot of information in a short time before the exam – which can cause anxiety and is not a reliable way to prepare.

UNDERSTAND THESE TERMS

- calibrated
- displacement
- immerse
- meniscus
- precise
- standard
- volume

1.2 Density

1   In this question, write each answer in words and in symbols.

   a   Write the equation used when calculating density.

   b   Write the unit of:

      i   a density calculated from a mass in grams and a volume in cubic centimetres

      ii   a mass calculated from a volume in m^3 and a density in kg/m^3

      iii   a volume calculated from a mass in kilograms and a density in kilograms per cubic decimetre.

   c   What is the density of water, in kg/m^3 and in g/cm^3?

   d   If you know the density of an object, how can you use it to predict whether the object will float in water?

   e   Why does ice float in water?

2   If liquid A floats on top of liquid B, what can you say about the densities of the two liquids?

3   Aerographene is an extremely low density material that was first created by scientists in the 2010s.

   A cube of aerographene has side length 10 cm, as shown in Figure 1.3.

10 cm

Figure 1.3

   a   Calculate the volume of the cube, writing the unit.   [2]

   b   The density of aerographene is $0.16\ mg/cm^3$. Show that the mass of the 10 cm cube is about 150 mg.   [3]

   c   Expanded polystyrene is a low density material that is used for packaging. It has a density of $20\ mg/cm^3$. Calculate the volume of expanded polystyrene, in cm^3, that would have the same mass as the 10 cm cube of aerographene.   [2]

   d   Aerographene contains many tiny holes. The cube of aerographene has density 0.16 mg/cm if these holes are empty, but it has a higher density if the holes are full of air. Suggest why.   [1]

[Total: 8]

4   A student finds a large old coin and he wants to find out what it is made from.

He finds the volume of the coin using the equipment shown in Figure 1.4.

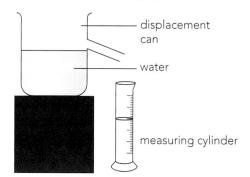

Figure 1.4

a   Describe how he can use this equipment to determine the volume
of the coin.   [2]

b   The student finds that the volume of the coin is 2.3 cm³.

He also knows that the mass of the coin is 24 g.

He thinks the coin is made from one of the materials in the table below.

Material	Density in g/cm³
brass	8.5
gold	19.3
lead	11.3
silver	10.5

State which of these metals the coin is most likely to be made from
and justify your answer.   [3]

c   Mercury is a metal that is a dense liquid at room temperature.

Objects that are made of lead float in mercury.

Using the information in the table above, predict whether an object
made of brass will float in mercury. Justify your answer.   [2]

[Total: 7]

> UNDERSTAND
> THESE TERMS
>
> • density
>
> • mass
>
> • weight

1.3 Measuring time

1   What differences are there between an analogue clock and a digital clock?

2   A plumb bob swings backwards and forwards. Each oscillation takes
approximately one second. How would you make an accurate measurement
of the period of the oscillations?

3   A boy is watching a spinning fairground ride. He wants to measure the time taken for each rotation. He uses an analogue watch to measure the time taken for seven complete rotations of the ride.

Figure 1.5 shows the watch at the start and end of the measurement.

Figure 1.5

a   Determine the time taken for one complete rotation of the fairground ride.   [2]

b   State one advantage of a digital stop-watch instead of an analogue watch for making a measurement like this.   [1]

c   Suggest one way to improve the accuracy of the measurement.   [1]

[Total: 4]

UNDERSTAND THESE TERMS

- analogue
- digital
- oscillation
- period
- plumb bob

SELF-ASSESSMENT CHECKLIST

Let's revisit the Knowledge focus and Exam skills focus for this chapter.

Decide how confident you are with each statement.

Now I can	Show it	Needs more work	Almost there	Confident to move on
take measurements of length, volume and time	Write a summary of the instruments and methods used to measure length, volume and time, and include the SI units for each quantity.			
perform experiments to determine the density of an object	Use the flip cards for this chapter to test yourself on your knowledge of methods for determining density.			

CONTINUED

Now I can	Show it	Needs more work	Almost there	Confident to move on
predict whether an object will float	Create a worksheet about this for other students to try and write a set of correct answers for it.			
predict whether one liquid will float on another	Write an exam-style question to test this. In the question, give liquid densities (or masses and volumes) and ask for the order of the liquid layers when they are all poured into a container. Write a mark scheme.			
show that I understand the command word 'determine' and can answer 'determine' questions.	Say what 'determine' means. After you have answered the 'determine' questions in this chapter, explain why that command word was chosen for those questions.			

2 Describing motion

KNOWLEDGE FOCUS

In this chapter, you will answer questions on:

- understanding speed
- distance–time graphs
- understanding acceleration
- calculating speed and acceleration.

EXAM SKILLS FOCUS

In this chapter you will:

- show that you understand the command word 'state' and can answer 'state' questions.

An important part of understanding exam questions is to know what command words are and what they mean. In this chapter you will practise answering questions that use the command word 'state'. It is important that you understand what command words are instructing you to do:

State	express in clear terms.

'State' questions may ask you to provide a fact or short answer in response to the question. For example, in this topic you may be asked to provide times of different events from a time-motion graph.

It is important not to provide too much information or detail when you answer these questions. You are not expected to provide detailed explanations or descriptions for this command word.

2.1 Understanding speed

1 a Find the average speed for each of the movements or journeys below, writing the answers in m/s.

    i In a school experiment, a moving trolley has an interrupt card attached to it. The length of the interrupt card is 0.15 m. As the trolley moves, the interrupt card passes through a light gate. The time it takes to do this is 0.3 s.

    ii When a person snaps their fingers, the tip of their middle finger travels 7 cm in 0.007 s.

    iii In 2014, Felix Baumgartner jumped from a helium balloon and fell a distance of 36 402 m in 4 minutes and 19 s without a parachute. (He did open his parachute for the last part of the fall!)

b i Monarch butterflies spend summer in North America and travel to Mexico for the winter. They complete this 4000 km journey in about 1400 hours (or about two months).

    ii During their 4000 km journey, monarch butterflies fly during the day and rest at night. Is their actual flying speed faster or slower than the average speed calculated above for the whole journey?

2 A car travels along a straight section of road between two speed cameras. Each camera records what time the car passes, and these measurements are used to check the car's speed. The distance between the cameras is 800 m.

    a A car passed the second camera 40 s after it passed the first camera. Calculate the average speed of the car between the two cameras, in m/s. [3]

    b The speed limit (maximum legal speed) on the road is 80 km/h. Show that the average speed of the car was less than this. [2]

    c While the car was driving between the cameras, it exceeded (went over) the speed limit. Explain how this is possible. [1]

    d Another car travels between the two cameras at a constant speed of 16 m/s. Calculate the time this takes. [3]

[Total: 9]

UNDERSTAND THESE TERMS
- average speed
- interrupt card
- light gates
- speed

≪ RECALL AND CONNECT 1 ≪

Using a ruler, how would you measure: the volume of a box in the shape of a cuboid, the thickness of one page of a book and the average diameter of a pea?

REFLECTION

Can you still remember what you learned about making measurements in Chapter 1? How do you know?

One way to check this is to try to answer Recall and connect questions like the one above. The Recall and connect questions do not test everything you need to know from previous chapters. How will you check that you remember other key terms and knowledge from chapters you have already worked on?

2.2 Distance–time graphs

1   A child is walking to school. She walks at a constant speed for 10 minutes. Then she stops to talk to a friend for 5 minutes. Then she realises she is late so she starts walking again, at a faster speed than before. She arrives at school 5 minutes later. Sketch a possible distance–time graph for this journey.

2   Two swimmers compete in a 20-metre race. Figure 2.1 shows the distance–time graphs for both swimmers.

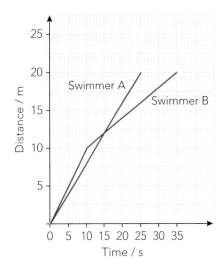

Figure 2.1

a   During the race, swimmer B became tired and slowed down. State the time at which this happened. [1]

b   State which swimmer has the higher speed during the first 10 s of the race. Explain how Figure 2.1 shows this. [2]

c   State the time at which one swimmer overtakes (passes) the other. [1]

d   Calculate the average speed of swimmer B. Include the unit in your answer. [4]

e   A third swimmer, swimmer C, swam in the race. He did not hear the start signal, and started swimming 5 seconds later than swimmers A and B. He took 25 seconds to swim the whole distance at a constant speed. On a copy of Figure 2.1, sketch a graph for this swimmer and label it 'Swimmer C'. [2]

f   State which of the three swimmers won the race and explain how the graphs show this. [2]

[Total: 12]

When marking your answer to 2d of this Exam skills question, did you notice that marks are given for writing the correct equation and for writing out your working? You can get these marks even if you get the final answer wrong (perhaps by typing it incorrectly into your calculator).

Can you think of any other reasons why it is useful to write working when you answer a calculation question?

Think about this when you answer calculation questions later in this chapter. You can use the mark scheme answers to help you check whether you are missing out any important steps.

2.3 Understanding acceleration

1   Figure 2.2 shows six graphs, A to F, with missing axes labels.

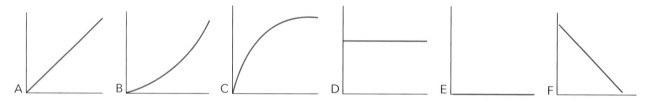

Figure 2.2: Six graphs without labels

   a   Which of graphs A to F could represent a distance–time graph for:

   i   an object that is not moving

   ii   an object that is moving at a constant speed

   iii an object that is accelerating

   iv   an object that is decelerating?

   b   Which of graphs A to F could represent a speed–time graph for:

   i   an object that is not moving

   ii   an object that is moving at a constant speed

   iii an object that is accelerating

   iv   an object that is decelerating?

2   **a**   What is the difference between speed and velocity?

   b   A feather is dropped and falls through the air at a constant speed. It falls a distance of 200 cm in 40 s.

   i   What is the speed of the feather?

   ii   What is the velocity of the feather?

3 In Figure 2.3, the letters A to H show the positions of the front of a car every 2 seconds as the car travels a distance of 100 m from left to right.

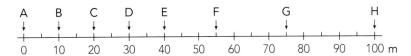

Figure 2.3

a Determine the distance travelled between C and F. [2]

b Determine the time taken for the car to travel from A to H. [1]

c Calculate the average speed of the car, in m/s, for the whole of the journey shown. [2]

d Describe the motion of the car between A and E. Explain how you know. [2]

e Describe the motion of the car between E and H. Explain how you know. [2]

f Sketch a distance–time graph for the journey shown in Figure 2.3. [2]

[Total: 11]

4 Supertankers are very large ships that transport oil. A supertanker travels at a steady speed of 24 km/h for 4.0 h and then takes 1.0 h to slow to a stop. While it is slowing down, its deceleration is constant.

a On a copy of Figure 2.4, sketch a speed–time graph for the supertanker. [2]

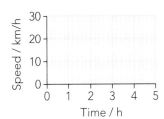

Figure 2.4

b Calculate the distance the supertanker travels, in km, from time = 0 h to time = 4.0 h. [2]

c At time = 4 h, the supertanker stops its engines. Calculate the distance it travels, in km, during the hour it takes to stop moving. [3]

d A cargo ship travels the same total distance as the first supertanker and takes the same time, but it travels at a constant speed. Calculate its speed in km/h. [4]

[Total: 11]

≪ RECALL AND CONNECT 2 ≪

If you want to predict whether a particular solid will float in a particular liquid, what information do you need? How would you use that information to make a prediction?

UNDERSTAND THESE TERMS

- acceleration
- scalar quantity
- vector quantity
- velocity

2.4 Calculating speed and acceleration

1 **a** Write the equation for acceleration in words.

b The acceleration equation can be written in symbols as $a = \dfrac{\Delta v}{\Delta t}$.
What does the symbol Δ mean?

c The equation for acceleration can also be written as $a = \dfrac{v - u}{t}$.
What do the symbols u and v mean?

d The maximum acceleration of a sports car is 9 m/s².
What does this tell you about how quickly the car's speed can change?

e Copy and complete the sentences using the words and phrases below.

| distance | speed | area under | gradient of |

Distance is the .... a ....–time graph. Speed is the
.... a ....–time graph. Acceleration is the ....
a ....–time graph.

2 Find the acceleration in each of the situations below. Write a suitable unit with each answer. (Do not convert any units.)

a A mantis shrimp punches its prey using its front claw. During a punch, the end of its claw accelerates from stationary to 23 m/s in 0.003 s.

b A horse, initially moving at a speed of 4 m/s, speeds up to 16 m/s in 5 s.

c A Formula One racing car accelerates from 0 to 100 km/h in 2.4 s.

3 Figure 2.5 shows the distance–time graph for a robot working in a factory.

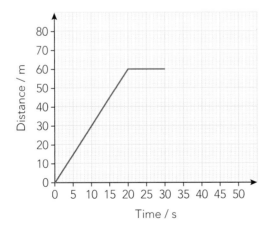

Figure 2.5

a Describe the motion shown for the first 20 s, calculating any relevant quantity. [3]

b Describe the motion, if any, of the robot between time = 20 s and time = 30 s. [1]

c   From time = 30 s to time = 50 s, the robot moves at a constant speed
    of 1 m/s. Draw an extension of the graph to show this.   [2]

[Total: 6]

4   A student drops a steel ball into a large measuring cylinder containing oil.
    She uses an electronic sensor to record the speed of the ball as it falls.
    Figure 2.6 shows the results.

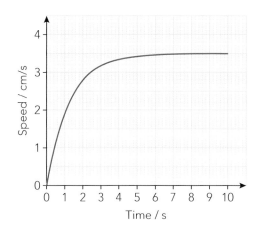

Figure 2.6

a   State and explain whether the density of the ball is higher or lower
    than the density of the oil.   [2]

b   Explain how the graph shows that the acceleration of the ball is
    not constant.   [1]

c   Describe the motion of the ball between time = 8 s and time = 10 s.   [1]

d   Using Figure 2.6, determine:

    i   the acceleration of the ball at time = 2.0 s   [3]

    ii the distance travelled by the ball between time = 8 s and time = 10 s.   [2]

[Total: 9]

SELF-ASSESSMENT CHECKLIST

Let's revisit the Knowledge focus and Exam skills focus for this chapter.

Decide how confident you are with each statement.

Now I can	Show it	Needs more work	Almost there	Confident to move on
define speed and calculate average speed	Check that you can recall the definition of speed and the equation for average speed.			

CONTINUED

Now I can	Show it	Needs more work	Almost there	Confident to move on
plot and interpret distance–time and speed–time graphs	Write two questions: one where you must draw a graph from a description, and one where you are given the graph and must describe what it shows. Ask a classmate to answer your questions. Mark their answers.			
work out the distance travelled from the area under a speed–time graph	Answer at least one exam-style question or real past exam question correctly using this skill.			
understand that acceleration is a change in speed and the gradient of a speed–time graph	On the same axes, sketch speed–time graphs showing objects with: a low acceleration, a high acceleration, a low deceleration, a high deceleration. Ask a teacher or classmate to check that your graphs are correct.			
distinguish between speed and velocity	Decide how you would explain this to a student who is three years younger than you.			
define and calculate acceleration; understand deceleration as a negative acceleration	Check that you can recall the definition of acceleration.			
show that I understand the command word 'state' and can answer 'state' questions.	Say what 'state' means. For each of the state questions in this chapter, explain why 'state' is a suitable command word for that question.			

3 Forces and motion

In this chapter you will practise answering questions that use the command word 'explain'. It is important that you understand what you must include in your answer to questions that include this command word.

| Explain | set out purposes or reasons/make the relationships between things evident/provide why and/or how and support with relevant evidence. |

Explanation questions usually ask for a longer response and are worth between 2 and 6 marks. Make sure you plan your answer to ensure all the points you need to include in your answer are covered. Be careful not to write a description instead of an explanation in your answer.

When asked to provide an explanation, give reasons for the data, or phenomenon, you are provided with. Be sure to state as much evidence as is necessary, from the question or from your own knowledge, to strengthen your answer.

3.1 We have lift-off

1   What happens to a moving object if the resultant force on it is:

    a   zero

    b   in the same direction as its motion

    c   in the opposite direction to its motion

    d   perpendicular (at right angles) to its motion?

2   Make a sketch to show how two forces could be applied to:

    a   stretch an object without changing its motion

    b   compress an object without changing its motion.

3   Figure 3.1 shows all of the forces that are acting on an object.

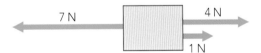

Figure 3.1

At the instant shown, the object is moving to the right.

    a   State the size and direction of the resultant force on the object.   [2]

    b   Describe the motion of the object.   [1]

    c   While the object is moving to the right, another force is now applied.
This force is 2 N and acts to the right. Describe and explain the motion,
if any, of the object just after this force starts to act.   [2]

        [Total: 5]

4   A child pushes a toy car along the floor at a constant speed.

    a   The child pushes with a constant force. Explain why the toy car does
not accelerate.   [2]

    b   The child now pushes with a larger force. The toy car accelerates.
Explain why.   [1]

    c   The child now releases the car. Describe and explain the motion
of the toy car after this.   [2]

        [Total: 5]

3.2 Mass, weight and gravity

1   What is the value and the unit of gravitational field strength, g, on Earth?

2   The value of g on another planet is 5.0 N/kg. On that planet, what is:

   a   the weight of an object with mass 8.0 kg

   b   the gravitational force on an object with mass 100 g

   c   the mass of an object with weight 30 kg

   d   the acceleration due to gravity?

3   In this question, assume the weight of 1.0 kg on Earth to be 9.8 N.

   a   Explain the difference between mass and weight. [2]

   b   A box is placed on a set of bathroom scales. The reading on the scales shows 5.0 kg. Calculate the weight of the box. [2]

A bathroom scales does not measure mass directly. It measures the size of the force pushing down on it. Its measuring scale is calibrated to show the size of the mass that would cause that force.

   c   A child places a bathroom scales on the floor and then pushes down on it with their hand. While they do this, the scales shows a reading of 6 kg. Calculate the size of the child's pushing force. [2]

A bathroom scales from Earth is taken to the Moon. The gravitational field strength is lower on the Moon than it is on Earth.

   d   A person with mass 60 kg stands on the scales on the Moon. Predict whether the scales will show the person's mass as: less than 60 kg, equal to 60 kg, or more than 60 kg. Explain your answer. [2]

   e   Explain why the bathroom scales cannot be used to measure mass in deep space (far from any planets). [1]

[Total: 9]

UNDERSTAND THESE TERMS

- air resistance
- drag
- forces
- friction
- newton (N)
- resultant force
- solid friction

REFLECTION

You may have noticed that there are not many facts (such as definitions and equations) to memorise for section 3.2 Mass, weight and gravity. However, these few facts are very important to know.

The Exam skills question 3b requires mathematical skills, while in parts c, d and e you need to apply your understanding to new situations. However, none of the question parts can be answered without also having some knowledge. What piece(s) of knowledge does each question part require?

If your recall of knowledge is good then it will improve your confidence and performance in the exam. How will you find and memorise the essential facts about mass, weight and gravity – and about the other areas of the Forces and motion topic?

UNDERSTAND THESE TERMS

- acceleration due to gravity
- acceleration of free fall
- gravitational field strength
- gravity

3.3 Falling and turning

1   BASE jumping means doing a parachute jump from a stationary object such as a cliff or tall building. Figure 3.2 shows a speed–time graph for a BASE jumper from the start to the end of their fall. Four times during the fall are labelled **i**, **ii**, **iii** and **iv**.

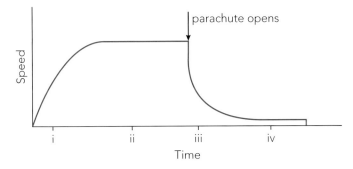

Figure 3.2: A speed–time graph for a falling BASE jumper

a   What term is used for the speed at which the jumper is falling at time **ii** on the graph?

Figure 3.3 shows the forces acting on the parachutist at the four times labelled on the graph.

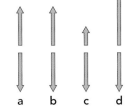

Figure 3.3: Forces acting on a BASE jumper at different times during the fall

b   Match each force diagram in Figure 3.3 to one of the four times labelled on the graph in Figure 3.2. Explain how you made your choices.

c   Sketch a speed–time graph for a falling object on a planet where there is no atmosphere, and therefore no air resistance.

2   A toy car travels around a circular track at constant speed. Figure 3.4 shows the position of the car at one instant.

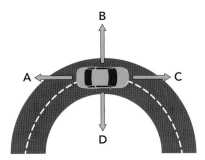

Figure 3.4: Toy car on a circular track

The car is travelling clockwise around the circle.

a Which of the arrows, labelled A, B, C and D, correctly shows the direction of:

  i the velocity of the car

  ii the acceleration of the car

  iii the resultant force acting on the car?

b The car is accelerating without changing its speed. How is this possible?

c Name the force that causes this acceleration.

3 A student drops a steel ball into a large measuring cylinder containing oil. She uses an electronic sensor to record the speed of the ball as it falls. Figure 3.5 shows the results.

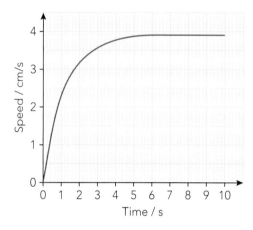

Figure 3.5

a State the direction of the resultant force on the ball at time = 2.0 s. [1]

b Figure 3.6 shows all of the forces acting on the ball at one instant during its fall. (Upthrust is the upward push of the oil on the ball.)

Identify the type of force represented by each of the arrows labelled A and B. [2]

c The upthrust force is constant throughout the fall. Describe how each of these forces changes, if at all, during the first 3 seconds of the fall:

  i force A [1]

  ii force B. [1]

d State the time at which the ball first reaches terminal velocity. [1]

e At time = 9.0 s, force B is 1.0 N and the upthrust on the ball is 0.20 N. Determine the size of force A at time = 9.0 s. [2]

[**Total: 8**]

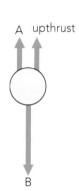

Figure 3.6

> **UNDERSTAND THIS TERM**
>
> • terminal velocity

3.4 Force, mass and acceleration

≪ RECALL AND CONNECT 3 ≪

A student is asked what acceleration is and gives the answer 'speeding up'. Give a better answer which shows that acceleration is a quantity that can be measured. Include an equation in your answer.

1   a   Say whether each of the statements below is true or false, and why.

      i   If equal resultant forces are applied to two objects of different mass, then the object with more mass has a larger acceleration.

      ii   If two objects have the same acceleration, the resultant forces on the objects must be equal.

      iii   For an object of constant mass, acceleration is directly proportional to resultant force.

   b   What resultant force would be needed to give a body of mass 2.0 kg an acceleration of 10 m/s^2?

   c   If a body has acceleration 8 m/s^2 when a resultant force of 4 N acts on it, what mass must the body have?

2   A cyclist exerts a forward force of 140 N on their bicycle, while there is a total backward force of 20 N on the bicycle due to friction. The total mass of the cyclist and the bicycle is 85 kg.

   a   Calculate the resultant force on the bicycle.   [1]

   b   Calculate the acceleration of the bicycle. Include the unit in your answer.   [3]

   c   The cyclist continues to apply the same forward force, but the bicycle's acceleration decreases. Suggest why.   [1]

[Total: 5]

3.5 Momentum

1   a   A child is standing on a frozen lake. They kick a small stone across the ice. It hits a second stone that is stationary and the two stones stick together. To predict the speed of the joined stones after the collision, what measurements would you need and how would you use them?

   b   Use the idea of impulse to explain why an egg breaks when it is dropped from a short height onto concrete but not when it is dropped from the same height onto a cushion.

2   A teacher demonstrates the collision of two carts on a straight horizontal track. The track is frictionless. The carts stick together when they collide.

Before the collision, one cart is stationary and the other cart is moving towards it at a speed of 0.6 m/s.

The mass of each cart is 0.5 kg.

a   Calculate the momentum of the moving cart before the collision. Include the unit in your answer.   [3]

b   Using the principle of the conservation of momentum, calculate the speed of the joined carts after the collision.   [3]

[Total: 6]

UNDERSTAND THESE TERMS

• collision
• impulse
• momentum
• principle of the conservation of momentum

3   A golfer uses a golf club to hit a ball. The mass of the ball is 45 g.

Before the ball is hit, it is stationary. Immediately afterwards, it is moving at a speed of 72 m/s.

a   Calculate the change in momentum of the golf ball, in kg m/s.   [3]

b   State the impulse given to the ball, in N s.   [1]

c   The club and ball are in contact for a time of 0.0005 s. Calculate the average force of the club on the ball during this time.   [3]

[Total: 7]

3.6 More about scalars and vectors

1   List five scalar quantities and five vector quantities.

2   Two bears are leaning against a tree. Figure 3.7 shows the trunk of the tree (from above) and the forces the bears exert on it. The forces are perpendicular to each other.

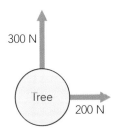

300 N

Tree

200 N

Figure 3.7

a   Calculate the magnitude of the resultant of the bears' forces, without making a scale drawing.   [3]

b   Determine the angle between the resultant force and the 200 N force.   [2]

[Total: 5]

UNDERSTAND THIS TERM

• vector triangle

SELF-ASSESSMENT CHECKLIST

Let's revisit the Knowledge focus and Exam skills focus for this chapter.

Decide how confident you are with each statement.

Now I can	Show it	Needs more work	Almost there	Confident to move on
outline the differences between mass and weight	Create a table of differences, including the definitions, the units, and whether they are affected by which planet an object is on.			
describe the ways in which a resultant force may change the motion of a body	Create a poster or cartoon showing all the ways in which a resultant force may change the motion of a body.			
find the resultant of two or more forces acting along the same line	Show a classmate how to do this.			
find out about the effect of friction (or air resistance or drag) on a moving object	Plan how you would teach this to students of your age who have not yet learned about it.			
describe circular motion	Write a summary, including one or more diagrams, of everything you think you should know about circular motion. Compare this with what the specification says about circular motion.			
explain how force, mass and acceleration are related	Recall the formulae that relates these quantities. Describe the effects on acceleration of changing the mass and resultant force.			
define what a force is, use the concepts of momentum and impulse and apply the principle of the conservation of momentum	Create a poster, mind map or slideshow about what momentum and impulse are and how to calculate them, and how to use the principle of conservation of momentum to answer questions.			
understand the difference between scalars and vectors and learn how to determine the resultant of two vectors acting at right angles to each other	Write an exam-style question that tests this objective. Give it to a classmate, and then mark their answer.			
show that I understand the command word 'explain' and can answer 'explain' questions.	Try past exam Questions 5b and c from Exam practice 1 that use the command word 'explain'. Use the example answers and commentary provided to check your answers.			

4 Turning effects

In this chapter you will practise answering questions that use the command word 'calculate'. It is important that you understand the meaning of this command word and what you need to do to answer questions that use it.

| Calculate | work out from given facts, figures or information. |

You must remember to show all the steps in your working when answering 'calculate' questions. This is because you may receive marks for using the correct method, even if you have used the wrong values in your answer. You should also include the correct units in your answer: remember not to confuse millimetres with centimetres, for example.

Practise showing all your working as you answer the 'calculate' questions in this chapter.

Many concepts in physics are connected to each other. For example, some of the questions in this chapter involve ideas from Forces and motion Chapter 3, because turning effects are caused by forces. It is common for an exam question to require knowledge and understanding of more than one concept or topic. As you practise answering questions, you will become more aware of this and develop your ability to connect different concepts.

4.1 The moment of a force

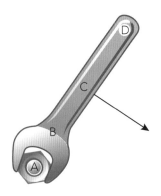

1   How can you tell by observation whether an object is in equilibrium?

2   A man uses a spanner to try to loosen a bolt. The force he exerts on the spanner is represented by an arrow in Figure 4.1.

    a   Identify the position of the pivot (A, B, C or D).   [1]

    b   State the direction of the moment produced by the man's force.   [1]

    c   The man does not succeed in making the spanner turn. Suggest why, using the idea of moments.   [2]

    d   Suggest two different ways the man could increase his turning effect.   [2]

[Total: 6]

Figure 4.1

《 RECALL AND CONNECT 1 《

What is the difference between mass and weight? What is the standard unit of each of these quantities?

UNDERSTAND THESE TERMS

- equilibrium
- moment
- pivot
- turning effect

4.2 Calculating moments

1   Figure 4.2 shows two situations in which a moment is used: using a crowbar to lift a heavy rock and using a wheelbarrow. The force is shown by an arrow in each picture.

Make a simple sketch of each picture. On each sketch:

- label the pivot

- draw an arrow to show the perpendicular distance between the force and the pivot.

Figure 4.2: Using moments

2   A child is playing with a toy seesaw.

As shown in Figure 4.3, she hangs a block of weight 8 N from the seesaw at 30 cm to the right of the pivot. Then she holds the seesaw so that it is horizontal.

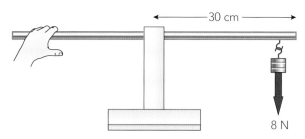

Figure 4.3: Toy seesaw held horizontally, with block of weight 8 N hanging from it at 30 cm from the pivot

a   In which direction does the seesaw rotate when the child stops holding it? Why?

The child wants to balance the seesaw by hanging one block to the left of the pivot. To balance the seesaw:

b   If the block has weight 10 N, how far from the pivot should she hang it to balance the seesaw?

c   If the block has weight 6 N, how far from the pivot should she hang it to balance the seesaw?

d   If she balances the seesaw by hanging a block 50 cm to the left of the pivot, what weight will the block have?

3   **a**   State the two conditions necessary for a body to be in equilibrium.   [2]

A uniform beam rests on a pivot at its centre. There are two objects resting on the beam, as shown in Figure 4.4.

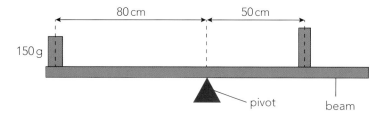

Figure 4.4

The beam is in equilibrium.

b   Calculate the weight of the 150 g object.   [2]

c   Calculate the moment of the 150 g object, in N cm, and state whether it is a clockwise or an anticlockwise moment.   [3]

d   Determine the weight of the object at 50 cm to the right of the pivot.   [3]

e   The pivot exerts a force on the beam. Calculate the size of this force and state its direction.   [3]

[Total: 13]

4 Figure 4.5 shows a type of decoration called a mobile, which hangs from a baby's bedroom ceiling.

The mobile has a light rod that hangs from the ceiling by a string. Three objects hang from the rod by strings; from left to right, these are: a star, a moon and a cloud.

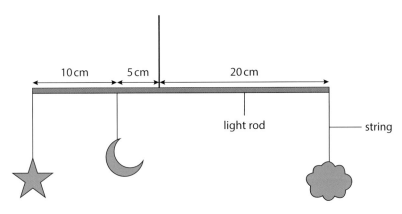

Figure 4.5

Since the rod is light, any moment caused by the rod's weight can be ignored.

a The mobile is in equilibrium, and the pivot is the point where the string attaches to the rod. The weight of the moon is 0.20 N and the weight of the cloud is 0.50 N.

Calculate the moment of the star, in N cm, about the pivot. [4]

b The string attached to the moon breaks. Describe and explain what happens to the mobile. [2]

c The child's parents decide to replace the moon with a different object: a sun. It has greater mass than the moon.

    i Identify the correct position to hang the sun to make the rod balance horizontally:

        A less than 5 cm from the pivot

        B exactly 5 cm from the pivot

        C more than 5 cm from the pivot.

    ii Explain your answer. [3]

d Another planet, called Planet Q, is smaller than Earth and its gravitational field strength is half that of Earth's. If the balanced mobile from Earth is taken to Planet Q and hung from a ceiling, predict whether it will still balance. Explain your answer. [3]

[Total: 12]

≪ RECALL AND CONNECT 2 ≪

a If an object has no resultant force acting on it, will it: be stationary, move at constant velocity, change its direction of motion or slow down?

b Describe the possible effects of a resultant force on an object.

UNDERSTAND THESE TERMS

- anticlockwise
- clockwise
- principle of moments

4.3 Stability and centre of gravity

1   Figure 4.6 shows two vases. The centre of gravity of each vase is marked with a cross (✗).

   a   Make a sketch of each vase rotated clockwise so that it is on the point of toppling. Which vase is more stable, and why?

   b   If either vase is rotated too far, it topples. Why does this happen? (Use the idea of moments in your answer.)

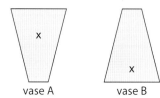

Figure 4.6: Two vases, each with its centre of gravity marked by a cross

2   Figure 4.7 shows a crane lifting a heavy load.

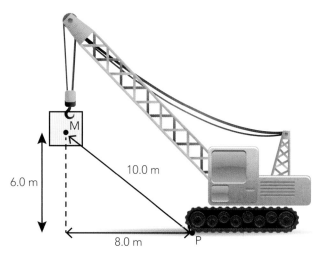

Figure 4.7

The point labelled P acts as a pivot.

   a   The crane has a low centre of gravity. Explain why this makes it stable.   [1]

   b   If the centre of gravity of the load is at the position marked M in Figure 4.7, calculate the maximum weight of the load for the crane not to topple.   [4]

[Total: 5]

REFLECTION

When you answered calculation questions in this chapter, what steps did you write in your answers?

If your final answer to a calculation exam question is correct, you will gain all of the marks available for the question (unless the question states 'show your working' and you do not). If your final answer is incorrect and you write nothing else, you will gain no marks. However, if you write an incorrect answer but also include one or more correct steps in your working, you may gain one or two marks.

Whenever you mark your answers to a calculate question, pay attention to how the marks are gained. Can you write a short set of instructions on how to answer calculate questions in the IGCSE Physics exam? Show your instructions to a classmate and share ideas.

UNDERSTAND THESE TERMS

- centre of gravity
- stable
- unstable

SELF-ASSESSMENT CHECKLIST

Let's revisit the Knowledge focus and Exam skills focus for this chapter.

Decide how confident you are with each statement.

Now I can	Show it	Needs more work	Almost there	Confident to move on
describe and calculate the turning force	Sketch three situations in which a force causes a moment. In each sketch, label the pivot and the perpendicular distance from the pivot.			
investigate and apply the principle of moments	Recall the principle of moments. Explain how it is possible for a seesaw to balance when two people with different weights are sitting on it.			
describe the conditions needed for an object to be in equilibrium	Recall the two conditions needed.			
describe how the centre of gravity of an object affects its stability	Find some everyday objects and say whether they are stable or unstable (which may vary depending on how they are positioned), and why.			

CONTINUED

Now I can	Show it	Needs more work	Almost there	Confident to move on
apply the principle of moments when there is more than one moment on each side of a pivot	Write an exam-style question to test this. Give it to a classmate and mark their answer.			
show that I understand the command word 'calculate' and can answer 'calculate' questions	Try at least two past paper questions that use this command word and check your answers. (You could try Questions 1b and 3 in Exam practice 1.)			
practise making connections between different concepts.	Find the Exam skills questions in this chapter that make connections between concepts from this chapter and previous chapters. Say which concepts are being tested.			

Exam practice 1

This section contains past paper questions from previous Cambridge exams, which draws together your knowledge on a range of topics that you have covered up to this point. These questions give you the opportunity to test your knowledge and understanding. Additional past paper practice questions can be found in the accompanying digital material.

The following question has an example student response and commentary provided. Once you have worked through the question, read the student response and commentary. Are your answers different to the sample answers?

1   Figure 1.1 shows a coil of wire.

   a   A student measures the length of the coil using a ruler.
His measurement is 3.8 cm.

There are 20 turns of wire in the coil. The student uses his measurement to calculate the average thickness of the wire.

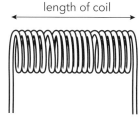

Figure 1.1 (not to scale)

     i   Show that the average thickness of the wire is about 0.2 cm.

          average thickness of wire = ... cm   [2]

     ii   The student's measurement of 3.8 cm is inaccurate.

         Suggest **one** reason why the measurement is inaccurate.   [1]

   b   The volume of the wire in the coil is 16.6 cm³ and its mass is 148 g.

     Calculate the density of the metal used for the wire in the coil.

                density = ... g/cm³   [3]

   c   The student has a measuring cylinder and a beaker of water, as shown in Figure 1.2

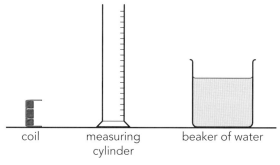

Figure 1.2

Describe how the student can determine the volume of the coil by using the equipment shown in Figure 1.2.   [4]

                                                   [Total: 10]

Cambridge IGCSE Physics, (0625) Paper 31, Q1, June 2020

Example student response	Commentary
1 a i average thickness = 0.19 cm	This is the correct thickness (and the student has not simply copied it from the question, because they have calculated it correctly to two significant figures). However, this is a 'show that' question, so to get both marks, the student also needs to show the calculation. *This answer is awarded 1 out of 2 marks.*
ii Maybe the student's eye was not level with the marking on the ruler	There are several possible correct answers to this suggest question, and the student has given one of them. *This answer is awarded 1 out of 1 mark.*
b $\rho = \dfrac{m}{v} = 16.6 \div 148 = 0.11$ g/cm³	The correct equation for density (in symbols or words) gains 1 mark. The student has substituted the measurements incorrectly, so does not gain any more marks. *This answer is awarded 1 out of 3 marks.*
c Half fill the measuring cylinder. Then put the coil into it so that it is covered with water. Read the volume of the coil.	This is an incomplete description, and not enough to get all 4 marks. The student gains 1 mark for each of the first two sentences. However, they have not described how to use readings from the measuring cylinder to calculate the volume of the wire. *This answer is awarded 2 out of 4 marks.*

2 Now that you've gone through the commentary, try to write an improved answer to the parts of the question where you lost marks. This will help you check if you've understood why each mark has (or has not) been allocated. Use the commentary to guide you as you answer.

The following question has an example student response and commentary provided.

Once you have worked through the question, read the student response and commentary. Are your answers different to the sample responses? What information does this give you about your understanding of this topic?

3 a Figure 3.1 shows a speed–time graph for a car.

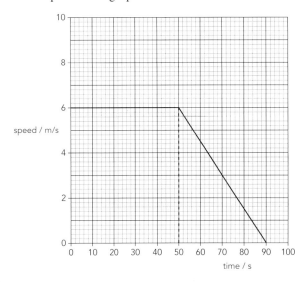

Figure 3.1

i   Describe the motion of the car from 0 to 50 s, as shown in Figure 3.1. [1]

ii Describe the motion of the car from 50 s to 90 s, as shown
in Figure 3.1.   [1]

iii Calculate the distance travelled by the car between 50 s and 90 s.

distance travelled = ... m   [3]

b   A motorcycle travels at constant speed.

i   The motorcycle travels 710 m in 87 s.

Calculate the speed of the motorcycle and show that it is close to 8 m/s. [3]

ii The motorcycle in part **b i** travels at a constant speed for 87 s.

On Figure 3.1, draw the speed–time graph for the motorcycle. [2]

[Total: 10]

Cambridge IGCSE Physics, (0625) Paper 31, Q1, June 2021

Example student response	Commentary
3 a i It is not moving	This statement would be true for a horizontal line on a distance–time graph, but it is not true for a horizontal line on a speed–time graph. *This answer is awarded 0 out of 1 mark.*
ii It is decelerating	This is correct. (A fuller description would be that the deceleration is constant, but it is not necessary to say that to get the mark.) *This answer is awarded 1 out of 1 mark.*
iii ½ × base × height = ½ × 90 × 6 = 270	The correct equation for the area of a triangle gains 1 mark. The student has used an incorrect number (90) in the working, so does not gain any more marks. *This answer is awarded 1 out of 3 marks.*
b i $v = s/t$ = 710 ÷ 87 = 8	The equation and working are correct. However, since the student has written the answer '8' and the question already states that the answer is 'close to 8', the student has not proved that they carried out the calculation correctly. To do this, they would need to write down at least one more significant figure in their answer. *This answer is awarded 2 out of 3 marks.*

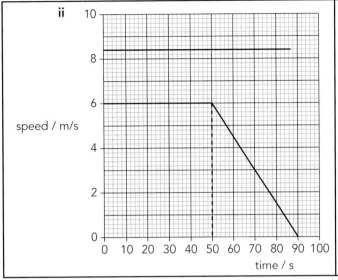

ii

The student's graph is a horizontal line, which is the correct shape to show constant speed. However, it shows a speed of 8.4 m/s instead of 8.2 m/s. (Note that each small vertical square represents 0.2 m/s.)

This answer is awarded 1 out of 2 marks.

4   Now that you've gone through the commentary, try to write an improved answer to the parts of the question where you lost marks. This will help you check if you've understood why each mark has (or has not) been allocated. Use the commentary to guide you as you answer.

The following question has an example student response and commentary provided. Once you have read and answered the question, read the student response and commentary. Are your answers different? If so, how are they different?

In this question, take the weight of 1.0 kg to be 10 N (acceleration of free fall = 10 m/s²).

5   A skydiver of mass 76 kg is falling vertically in still air. At time $t = 0$, the skydiver opens his parachute.

Figure 5.1 is the speed–time graph for the skydiver from $t = 0$.

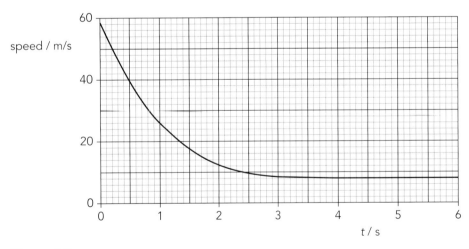

Figure 5.1

a   Using Figure 5.1, determine:

     i   the deceleration of the skydiver immediately after the parachute opens   [2]

     ii   the force due to air resistance acting on the skydiver immediately
        after the parachute opens.   [3]

b   Explain, in terms of the forces acting on the skydiver, his motion
    between $t = 0$ and $t = 6.0$ s.   [3]

c   Explain why opening the parachute cannot reduce the speed of
    the skydiver to zero.   [2]

[Total: 10]

Cambridge IGCSE Physics, (0625) Paper 41, Q1, June 2021

Example student response	Commentary
5 **a** **i** 58	The student has read the speed from the graph when the parachute opens (at $t = 0$). This is not the same as the acceleration. *This answer is awarded 0 out of 2 marks.*
ii F = ma = 76 × 58 = 4408 N	The student has correctly evaluated F = ma using the mass and their incorrect value of acceleration from part **a**. This gains 1 mark. However, the result of this calculation is the resultant force on the skydiver, which does not equal the force due to air resistance. The student has failed to allow for skydiver's weight. *This answer is awarded 1 out of 3 marks.*
b The skydiver decelerates at a decreasing rate, and reaches a steady speed of 8 m/s after about 3.5 s.	The student has given a correct description of the motion, but the question asks for an explanation. *This answer is awarded 0 out of 3 marks.*
c Opening the parachute makes the air resistance large, and it is bigger than the weight. Therefore there is a resultant force upwards. So the skydiver decelerates and this makes the air resistance decrease, so the resultant force decreases. While this happens, the skydiver has a deceleration which is decreasing in size. Eventually the resultant force is zero and there is no more deceleration, but the skydiver still has some speed at this point and so continues to fall at the speed they were going when the acceleration stopped.	This answer includes the key points, although it is longer and more detailed than necessary. *This answer is awarded 2 out of 2 marks.*

6   Now write an improved answer to parts of this question where you lost marks.
This will help you check if you've understood why each mark has (or has not)
been allocated. Use the commentary to guide you as you answer.

The following question has an example student commentary and answer provided. Work through the question first, than compare your answer to the sample answer and commentary. How different were your answers to the example student answers? Are there any areas where you feel you need to improve your understanding?

Note that 'centre of mass' has the same meaning as centre of gravity. The current exam specification does not require you to know the term 'centre of mass'.

7   a   A student determines the centre of mass of a piece of wood. The wood is an irregular shape of constant thickness.

He suspends the piece of wood from a nail as shown in Figure 7.1. The wood is able to swing freely.

The student suspends a weight on a thin string from the nail.

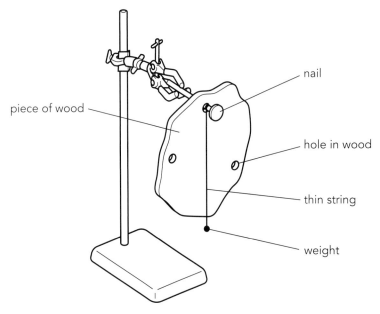

Figure 7.1

Describe how to determine the centre of mass of the piece of wood in Figure 7.1.

You may draw a diagram to help your answer.   [3]

   b   Figure 7.2 shows a flat, symmetrical object. Indicate its centre of mass by drawing X in the correct position.   [1]

Figure 7.2

c Figure 7.3 shows a side view of a drinking-glass in two different positions, A and B.

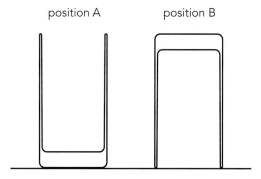

position A   position B

Figure 7.3

State which position, A or B, is more stable. Explain your answer.   [2]

[Total: 6]

Cambridge IGCSE Physics, (0625) Paper 32, Q5, November 2021

Example student response	Commentary
7 **a** Draw a line on the wood behind the string. Repeat. The centre of mass is where the lines cross.	Although drawing a line behind the string is a correct step, the student has not included enough detail about how to do this, so this does not gain a mark. The student has written 'repeat' but has not described what needs to be changed before repeating the first step. This does not gain a mark. It is correct that the centre of mass is where the lines cross (as long as the lines have been drawn using a correct method). This step gains a mark. *This answer is awarded 1 out of 3 marks.*
b X	The position is on the line of symmetry (the vertical mirror line) and is close enough to the 'navel' of the figure to get the mark. *This answer is awarded 1 out of 1 mark.*
c A because the glass has a larger surface area in contact with the ground.	The student has given the correct position for an incorrect reason. *This answer is awarded 1 out of 2 marks.*

8 Now that you've gone through the commentary, try to write an improved answer to parts of the question where you lost marks. This will help you check if you've understood why each mark has (or has not) been allocated. Use the commentary to guide you as you answer.

5 Forces and matter

In this chapter you will practise answering questions that use the command word 'predict'.

When you are asked to 'predict', you will usually need to use your knowledge and understanding of physics together with the information given in the question.

| Predict | suggest what may happen based on available information. |

'Predict' questions can be challenging. They require you to use knowledge and information from the question to produce an answer which is not always immediately obvious. Sometimes, 'predict' questions are combined with the instructional word 'justify'. For example, 'Predict… and justify your answer'. Write your response to the command word and then justify it – that is, show why or how you chose your response.

5.1 Forces acting on solids

1 Name as many ways as you can in which an object can deform.

2 a An object is acted on by only one force, which is constant. Which one of the following is possible? [1]

   A The object stretches.
   B The object twists.
   C The object slows down.
   D The object moves at constant velocity.

  b A second force is now applied to the object. It is the same size as the first force. Which one of the following is **not** possible? [1]

   A The object bends.
   B The object compresses.
   C The object slows down.
   D The object moves at constant velocity.

5.2 Stretching springs

1 A spring is hung so that its top end is fixed. Increasing amounts of weight are hung from the end of the spring, until the spring becomes permanently stretched.

  a Make a sketch of a graph showing the load on the *y*-axis and the extension of the spring on the *x*-axis.

  b Make another graph sketch, this time showing the extension on the *y*-axis and the load on the *x*-axis. (Graphs for this type of experiment are sometimes drawn this way.)

2 Make a labelled sketch to show the apparatus used to measure the extension of a spring under different loads.

3 A student carries out an experiment to determine the effect of different loads on a spring.

  a Give one reason why the student should wear eye protection. [1]

The student measures the total length of the spring when it is stretched by increasingly large forces.

They plot force on the *y*-axis and total length of the spring on the *x*-axis. Figure 5.1 shows their graph.

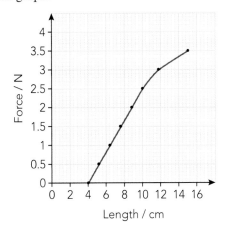

Figure 5.1

b   State the original length of the spring when it is not extended and justify your answer. [2]

c   On a copy of the same axes, draw a force–extension graph for the spring for forces up to 2.5 N. [1]

d   Describe the relationship between force and extension for the spring, when

  i   the force is less than 2.5 N [1]

  ii   the force is greater than 2.5 N. [1]

e   Another student repeats the experiment using the same spring, correctly following the same method as the first student. Explain why the second student's graph will not be the same as the first student's graph. [1]

[**Total: 7**]

UNDERSTAND THESE TERMS

- extension
- load

≪ RECALL AND CONNECT 1 ≪

a   When trying to turn a level or handle that is very stiff, how can you make sure your turning effect is large?

b   What does it mean for an object to be in equilibrium?

5.3 The limit of proportionality and the spring constant

1 a   Write the Hooke's law equation in words and in symbols.

   b   A spring has spring constant 2.0 N/cm. The spring extends by 9.0 cm when an object is hung from it. What is the force on the object?

   c   Two springs, A and B, have different spring constants. Spring B has a higher spring constant than spring B. Which spring requires more force to produce the same extension?

   d   Figure 5.2 shows a sketch of a load–extension graph for a spring.

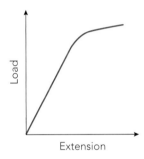

Figure 5.2

   i   Find the limit of proportionality on the graph. What happens to the spring at higher loads than this?

   ii   Continue the graph to show what happens when the maximum load is completely removed.

2 Figure 5.3 shows the load–extension graph for a spring.

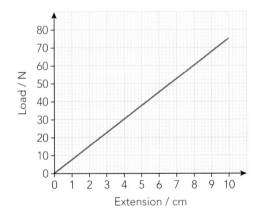

Figure 5.3

   a   Describe two features of the graph that show that the spring obeys Hooke's law.   [2]

   b   Determine the spring constant of the spring. Write the unit with your answer.   [3]

One end of the spring is fixed and the other end is attached to a beam, as shown in Figure 5.4. The beam is uniform and the pivot is at its centre.

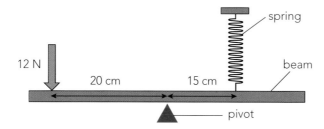

Figure 5.4

c The beam is in equilibrium. Calculate the extension of the spring. [5]

[Total: 10]

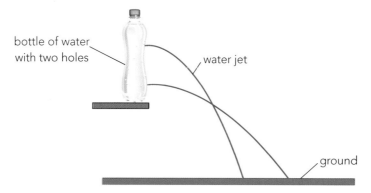

UNDERSTAND THESE TERMS
• limit of proportionality
• spring constant

5.4 Pressure

1 Decide whether each of the following statements is true or false.

a If an object is completely underwater, the pressure on the top of the object is greater than the pressure on the sides of the object.

b In a gas, the pressure increases as the depth increases.

c The denser the liquid, the greater the pressure it exerts.

d The pressure on an object in a fluid is caused by particles of the fluid hitting the object.

2 Why does pressure increase with depth in a liquid?

3 A bottle is filled with water and placed on a table. Two holes of equal size are made in the bottle, at different heights. A jet of water comes out of each hole, as shown in Figure 5.5.

Figure 5.5

a   The jet from the lower hole does not have as far to fall as the jet from the higher hole. However, the lower jet lands further away from the bottle. Explain why.   [1]

b   The water is replaced with acetone, a liquid that has a lower density than water.

Predict whether the jets of acetone will land on the ground nearer to the bottle than the water jets, or further away, and justify your answer.   [2]

c   Another bottle is full of water and the bottle's cap is screwed on tightly.

A pin is used to make only one small hole in the side of the bottle, below the level of the water surface.

No water flows out of the hole. Suggest why.   [2]

[Total: 5]

REFLECTION

How confident are you that you know what 'justify' means? Look back at your answer to the justify Question 3b and make sure you have explained how you chose your prediction.

5.5 Calculating pressure

1   Each of the statements below contains an error. Rewrite each statement so that it is correct.

a   The pressure on an object is the force acting per unit volume of the object.

b $1 \, N/cm^2 = 100 \, N/m^2$, because $1 \, m^2 = 100 \, cm^2$.

c   If an object rests on a table and the object's weight is $20 \, N$ and base area is $20 \, cm^2$, the pressure exerted by the object on the table, in pascals, is $1 \, Pa$.

2   The atmospheric pressure at the surface of the planet Venus is approximately $9 \times 10^6 \, Pa$. The atmospheric pressure at the surface of Earth is about $1 \times 10^5 \, Pa$.

a   How many times greater than the atmospheric pressure on Venus than the atmospheric pressure on Earth?

b   What is the force exerted by the atmosphere on each square centimetre of the ground:

i   on Earth

ii   on Venus?

3 A hammer is used to hit a nail into a piece of wood.

   a The head (top) of the nail is circular with a radius of 3.0 mm.
Show that the area of the head is approximately 28 mm². [1]

The hammer hits the head of the nail with a force of 400 N, and the nail hits the wall with a force of 400 N.

The sharp end of the nail has area 0.5 mm².

   b Calculate the pressure exerted by the hammer on the nail, in N/mm². [2]

   c The area of the sharp end of the nail is area 50 times smaller than the area of the head of the nail. Calculate the pressure exerted by the nail on the wall, in N/mm². [1]

   d A balloon bursts if it is pressed firmly onto the sharp point of a drawing pin (thumb tack).

      However, an identical balloon does **not** burst if it is pressed equally firmly onto a large number of drawing pins arranged on a table with their sharp points upwards. Explain why the balloon does not burst when pressed onto a large number of drawing pins at the same time. [2]

[Total: 6]

≪ RECALL AND CONNECT 2 ≪

   a Sketch a design for a drinking glass that is very stable.
Explain why it is stable.

   b Sketch a design for a drinking glass that is very unstable.
Explain why it is unstable.

UNDERSTAND THESE TERMS

- pascal
- pressure

REFLECTION

What mathematical skills did you need to use when answering in Question 3? Did you have any difficulties, and if so, what areas of maths will you need to work on?

One of the most common applications of mathematics in physics is working with equations. Do you need to learn any special methods for rearranging physics equations – or can you use the same methods that you have learned for rearranging formulae in your maths studies?

SELF-ASSESSMENT CHECKLIST

Let's revisit the Knowledge focus and Exam skills focus for this chapter.

Decide how confident you are with each statement.

Now I can	Show it	Needs more work	Almost there	Confident to move on
recognise that a force may change the size and shape of a body	Sketch the forces that would need to be applied to a cuboid made of sponge to make it do each of the following without accelerating: stretch, compress, twist, bend.			
plot and interpret load–extension graphs and describe the associated experimental procedure	Write a plan for an experiment to investigate the relationship between load and extension for a spring. Sketch how you expect the graph to look.			
recognise the significance of the 'limit of proportionality' for a load–extension graph	Sketch a load–extension graph and mark the limit of proportionality. Describe how the spring behaves at higher loads, and how it will behave if it is released.			
relate pressure to force and area and recall the associated equation $p = \dfrac{F}{A}$	Think of two objects that are designed to exert a low pressure for a reason (such as snowshoes) and two objects designed to exert a high pressure and explain how they achieve this. For one of the objects, find out typical values of area and force and calculate the pressure.			
relate the pressure beneath a liquid surface to depth and to density	Describe how pressure changes when depth increases, and when the density of the liquid increases.			

CONTINUED

Now I can	Show it	Needs more work	Almost there	Confident to move on
show that I understand the command word 'predict' and can answer 'predict' questions.	Create a two-minute presentation to show other students how to answer 'predict' questions.			

6 Energy stores and transfers

As you work through the Exam skills questions in the chapters, and in the Exam practice sections, notice how the marks are allocated. It is a useful habit to look at the number of marks available for each question (or part of a question) before you answer it. This can help you decide how best to answer. For example, if a question is worth three marks, you cannot get full marks by writing just one or two words, or by making one brief point. If a question is worth one mark, you should not need to write a paragraph. In a calculation question, the number of marks may give you a hint about how long the correct calculation will be (for example, do you need to rearrange an equation, or convert any units?).

When you practise past exam questions, use the mark schemes to check your answers and notice how the marks are allocated. You may be surprised how short some answers can be and still gain full marks – the important thing is that the key points are included clearly and correctly.

6.1 Energy stores

1 Name at least six types of energy store.

2 A battery-powered drone flies horizontally through the air at a constant speed. The temperature of the drone is constant.

    a For each of the drone's energy stores below, state whether the amount of energy stored is constant, increasing or decreasing, and explain how you know:

        i kinetic [2]

        ii gravitational potential [2]

        iii internal [2]

        iv chemical [2]

        v nuclear. [2]

    b The drone suddenly stops working, and it starts to fall freely.

       Describe the changes to its kinetic and gravitational potential energy stores as it starts to fall. [2]

[Total: 12]

« RECALL AND CONNECT 1 «

A student carries out an investigation of the relationship between load and extension for a spring.

a Define 'load' and 'extension'.

b The student continues increasing the load until the spring becomes permanently deformed. Sketch a graph showing the relationship between load and extension for a spring. Label the limit of proportionality.

c How can the student use their graph to find the spring constant of the spring?

UNDERSTAND THESE TERMS

- chemical energy
- doing work
- electromagnetic radiation
- gravitational potential energy (g.p.e.)
- internal energy
- kinetic energy
- nuclear energy
- thermal energy
- strain energy/ elastic energy

6.2 Energy transfers

1 Four methods of energy transfer are: electrical, thermal (or heating), radiation and mechanical. Categorise each of the transfers below into one of these four types:

    a a person stretches a spring (without permanently deforming it)

    b light travels from the Sun to the Earth

    c the wind makes a wind turbine turn

    d a battery makes a torch light up

    e a metal spoon becomes warm when it is used to stir hot soup

    f a toy car slows down and stops after being pushed by a child.

2   **a**   Identify the energy transfers and stores in each of the situations described below. Choose from the following list. (Each item in the list may be used once, more than once or not at all.)

| chemical | electrical | radiation | strain | kinetic |
| mechanical | gravitational potential | internal | | |

   i   When a rubber band is stretched, ... energy transfer increases the .... energy store of the rubber band.   [2]

   ii   When warm water is put into a cold glass, ... energy transfer decreases the .... energy store of the water and increases the .... energy store of the glass.   [3]

   iii   When a battery-powered car travels uphill at constant speed, ... energy transfer decreases the .... energy store of the battery. At the same time, ... energy transfer increases the .... energy store of the car.   [4]

   b   The temperature of the water at the bottom of a waterfall is usually slightly higher than the temperature of the water at the top. Explain why.   [2]

[Total: 11]

REFLECTION

Did you notice the number of marks available for part b of Question 2? When you answered it, did you think about how to gain both marks?

A two-mark answer to an 'explain' or 'describe' question should usually include two concepts, points or details. If 2b had been a one-mark question, what answer(s) do you think would gain the mark?

UNDERSTAND THESE TERMS

- event
- process

≪ RECALL AND CONNECT 2 ≪

a   A football player has weight 600 N. When they wear shoes, the total area of each shoe in contact with the ground is 200 cm². When they wear studded football boots, the total area of each shoe in contact with the ground is 20 cm².

   Find the pressure on the ground, in $\frac{N}{cm^2}$, when the footballer stands on one foot:

   i   when wearing shoes

   ii   when wearing football boots.

b   Convert your answers to part **a** into pascals.

c   Why do football boots have studs?

6.3 Conservation of energy

1   The table shows information about two different microwave ovens when they are each used for 10 s.

Microwave oven	Electrical energy transferred to device / J	Useful energy transferred by microwave radiation / J
Model A	10 000	8570
Model B	10 000	7083

Without doing a calculation, say which model is more efficient.
How do you know?

2   a   A torch transfers 85 J as heat and 15 J as light for every 100 J transferred from its battery's chemical energy store. Make a labelled sketch of a Sankey diagram for the torch.

b   To provide light, a torch must continuously transfer energy. As soon as the torch is switched off, the light disappears. What has happened to the light energy?

3   A student has a small toy wind turbine that is attached to a rechargeable battery. The student blows on the turbine, which makes it turn. As the turbine turns, it recharges a battery.

Figure 6.1 shows an energy flow diagram for this system. Energy stores are shown in dark boxes and energy transfers in light boxes.

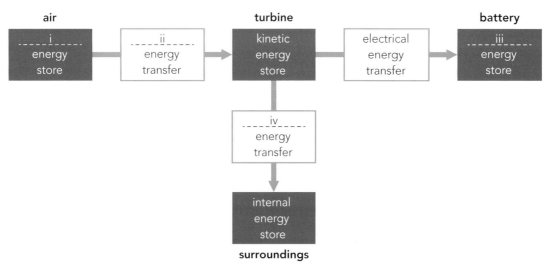

Figure 6.1

a   Four of the box labels are not completed. For each one, identify the missing energy store or transfer.   [4]

b For every 6 J of kinetic energy of the air blown by the student, 3 J is transferred to the battery's useful energy store. Calculate how much energy is wasted. [1]

c The student notices that the turbine sticks slightly as it turns. They use a small amount of oil to lubricate the moving parts of the turbine. After this, the turbine turns more easily. [2]

State and explain how this affects the efficiency of the system.

The student uses the rechargeable battery to power a small electric fan.

They discover that they can position the fan so that it blows on the wind turbine, which makes it turn, recharging the battery that powers the fan.

d The student thinks that the fan and the turbine will keep turning forever. Explain why this is not true (even if none of the parts break or wear out). [2]

[Total: 9]

4 **a** Describe the relationship between the total energy input and the total energy output of a device. [1]

b Give the name of the principle described in part **a**. [1]

c Figure 6.2 shows a Sankey diagram for a loudspeaker. The diagram is drawn to scale, so that the thicknesses of the arrows represent amounts of energy.

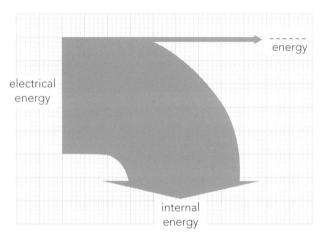

Figure 6.2

Complete the missing label. [1]

d Determine the efficiency of the loudspeaker. [2]

e Calculate the useful energy if the amount of electrical energy transferred to the loudspeaker is 300 J. [1]

f Use information from Figure 6.2 to explain why a loudspeaker that uses electrical energy quickly is likely to get hot. [1]

[Total: 7]

5 Figure 6.3 shows an example of the energy transfers that happen when a mobile phone is charged fully using a cable and then used until the battery runs out.

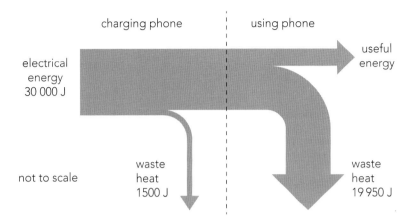

Figure 6.3

a State one way that useful energy is transferred by the phone. [1]

b Calculate the useful energy transferred by the phone. [1]

c Calculate the efficiency of the whole process (including both the charging and the phone use). [2]

d A wireless mobile phone charger has 70% efficiency when it is used to charge a mobile phone. Compare this with the efficiency of the cable phone charger used in Figure 6.3. [3]

[Total: 7]

6.4 Energy calculations

1 **a** Write the equation for calculating kinetic energy and write the SI unit of each of the quantities in the equation.

b Write the equation for calculating change in gravitational potential energy and write the SI unit of each of the quantities in the equation.

2 A student uses an electric motor to lift up a load. The student measures the electrical energy input to the motor while it is lifting the load, and finds that it is 25.0 J.

The load has mass 500 g and the motor lifts it by 1.00 m.

a Calculate the change in gravitational potential energy when the load is lifted. [3]

b Calculate the energy wasted when the load is lifted. [1]

c Calculate the efficiency of the motor when lifting this load. [2]

d Identify one energy store that the wasted energy transfers into. [1]

[Total: 7]

3 A plumb bob of mass 0.060 kg hangs on the end of a string in position B as shown in Figure 6.4. It is pulled to side and held in position A, which is 10 cm higher.

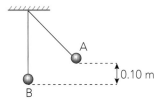

Figure 6.4

a Calculate the potential energy gained by the plumb bob when it is moved from B to A.   [2]

b The plumb bob is released and swings downwards through position B. Calculate the maximum speed the plumb bob could have when it reaches B.   [3]

The plumb bob passes through position B and continues swinging towards the left.

c The highest position reached by the plumb bob on the left side cannot be higher than position A. Explain why.   [2]

d Explain why the highest position reached on the left is likely to be lower than position A.   [1]

[Total: 8]

REFLECTION

Did you get both marks for Question 3 part c? Can you see why the response 'because of the principle of conservation of energy' would not be enough to gain 2 marks?

Would you have answered part d differently if it had been worth 2 marks?

SELF-ASSESSMENT CHECKLIST

Let's revisit the Knowledge focus and Exam skills focus for this chapter.

Decide how confident you are with each statement.

Now I can	Show it	Needs more work	Almost there	Confident to move on
identify changes in different energy stores	List and define all the energy stores that you have learned about.			

CONTINUED

Now I can	Show it	Needs more work	Almost there	Confident to move on
recognise different energy transfers and interpret energy flow diagrams	Draw an energy flow diagram, for a bungee jumper from the start to the lowest point of their jump, showing energy stores and transfers between them.			
understand the meaning of energy efficiency	Work out how you would explain the concept of efficiency to a younger student. If you are studying the supplement syllabus, answer a Exam practice question that asks you to calculate an efficiency.			
apply the principle of conservation of energy	Write an exam-style question that requires students to use the principle.			
calculate potential energy and kinetic energy	Write the formula for calculating each of these quantities, in symbols and in words.			
look at the number of available marks and write answers of appropriate length and detail.	Discuss with a classmate whether your answers to the exams skills questions were influenced by the number of marks available.			

7 Energy resources

55 >

KNOWLEDGE FOCUS

In this chapter, you will answer questions on:

- the energy we use

> energy from the Sun.

EXAM SKILLS FOCUS

In this chapter you will:

- show that you understand the command word 'give' and can answer 'give' questions.

In this chapter you will practise answering questions that use the command word 'give'. Questions with the 'give' command word require a short answer, usually a word(s) or a statement. Make sure you know what the command word is asking you to do. When you attempt the 'give' questions in this chapter, think about whether you fully understand what this command word means and what is required in answers to questions containing this command word.

| Give | produce an answer from a given source or recall/memory. |

7.1 The energy we use

1   Here are the main processes, in order, which take place in some types of power station:

1. Burn fuel → 2. Heat water to form fast-moving steam → 3. Turbine spins →

4. Spinning turbine operates generator → 5. Energy is transferred electrically

a   Which types of power station use all of these processes?

b   Which of the processes above **do not** take place when energy is generated:

   i   by geothermal power stations

   ii   by hydroelectric power stations

   iii   by solar cells?

2   List six factors to consider when comparing energy resources.

3   a   Give the name of the type of power station that transfers energy from hot underground rocks.   [1]

   b   Give two advantages of using nuclear power stations instead of solar cells to produce electricity.   [2]

   c   Give two advantages of using hydroelectric power stations instead of nuclear power stations to produce electricity.   [2]

[Total: 5]

4   Plants can be grown and then burned as biofuels, either in power stations or in the home.

   a   State where the energy stored in the biofuel comes from originally.   [1]

   b   Copy and complete the flow diagram by identifying the energy stores and energy transfers involved when wood is grown and then burned to heat a room.   [4]

   .... energy (transfer) → .... energy (store) of wood →

   .... energy (transfer) → .... energy (store) of room

   c   Plants absorb carbon dioxide from the air as they grow. Use this to explain why burning biofuels is less harmful to the environment than burning fossil fuels.   [2]

[Total: 7]

UNDERSTAND THESE TERMS

- biofuel
- boiler
- fossil fuels
- generator
- geothermal energy
- non-renewables
- nuclear fission
- renewables
- solar panel
- solar cell/photocell/photovoltaic cell
- turbine

7.2 Energy from the Sun

1   a   List the energy resources that get their energy from the Sun.

    b   List the energy resources that do not get their energy from the Sun.

2   Nuclear fusion is not yet a useful energy resource on Earth, but research is being carried out to try to make it possible.

    a   State one advantage of nuclear fusion compared with nuclear fission.   [1]

    b   Give one reason it is difficult to create a nuclear fusion power station.   [1]

[Total: 2]

≪ RECALL AND CONNECT 2 ≪

400 J of energy is transferred electrically to an electric fan but the fan only transfers 80 J to useful energy. Explain how this is consistent with the principle of conservation of energy and work out the efficiency of the fan.

UNDERSTAND THESE TERMS

- nuclear fusion
- water cycle

SELF-ASSESSMENT CHECKLIST

Let's revisit the Knowledge focus and Exam skills focus for this chapter.

Decide how confident you are with each statement.

Now I can	Show it	Needs more work	Almost there	Confident to move on
describe how electricity or other useful stores of energy may be obtained from different energy resources	Create a mind map, cartoon or poster summarising how each energy resource is used to obtain useful energy.			
give advantages and disadvantages of each energy resource in terms of renewability, cost, reliability, availability, scale and environmental impact	Without referring to a book or notes, make a table of energy resources, with columns showing any advantages or disadvantages for each of the six resources. Use your coursebook to check whether you missed any.			
understand that the Sun is the source of energy for all our energy resources except geothermal, nuclear and tidal	For each energy resource, explain to a younger friend or a family member where the energy originally comes from.			
understand that energy is released by nuclear fusion in the Sun	Check that you always remember that it is fusion, not fission, that takes place in the Sun. Describe the conditions needed for nuclear fusion to occur.			
show that I understand the command word 'give' and can answer 'give' questions.	Write two one-mark 'give' questions about energy resources. Write the answers.			

8 Work and power

In this chapter you will practise answering questions that use the command word 'define'. You should be able to understand what this command word is asking you to do.

Define	give precise meaning.

Ideally, you should answer a 'define' question by using the definition stated in the coursebook or syllabus. You can write it in your own words but you run the risk of being less precise than required. It is a good idea to practise writing the definitions for the key terms in the coursebook chapters as these are the terms you could be asked to define in an exam.

When it comes to preparing for exams, it helpful to know where you need to improve your knowledge or understanding. To improve your knowledge, you should spend time actively memorising (for example, by testing yourself using question and answer cards). To improve your understanding, you might find it helpful to read a textbook (and perhaps make summary notes or a mind map), watch online videos about physics topics, discuss ideas with classmates, or ask your teacher questions. To improve your ability to answer questions, you should work on practice questions – particularly exam questions.

8.1 Doing work

1 Give two examples of forces doing work. In each case, name the type of force.

2 **a** Define the term 'work done'. [1]

In a room there are two shelves. The first shelf is 2 m above the floor and the second shelf is 3 m above the floor.

b A box is lifted from the floor to the first shelf. Explain why work is done in this situation. [1]

c The box is then lifted from the first shelf to the second shelf. Identify which of these two actions requires more work:

A lifting the box from the floor to the first shelf

B lifting the box from the first shelf to the second shelf.

Explain your answer. [2]

[Total: 4]

« RECALL AND CONNECT 1 «

For each pair of energy resources below, write one advantage of the first compared with the second, and one advantage of the second compared with the first.

a solar panels and solar cells

b tidal power and wave power

c wind power and nuclear fission

UNDERSTAND THIS TERM

• work done

REFLECTION

When you revise this topic, how much time and effort do you think you will need to spend on: developing your knowledge, developing your understanding, and developing your ability to apply these when answering questions? How will you decide, and will you change this balance for different topics?

8.2 Calculating work done

1 **a** What is the SI unit of energy?

b Why does work done have the same SI unit as energy?

c Write an equation in symbols that relates work and force.

d A person uses a force of 20 N to pull a sledge a distance of 300 m. How much work is done by the person?

2 What are the two ways of calculating the work done when a force F is used to lift an object of mass m by a height h?

3 For each of the following situations, state and explain whether work is done:

   a lifting an object upwards   [2]

   b holding an object up in the air at a constant height   [2]

   c swinging an object in a circle on the end of a string.   [2]

                                                         [Total: 6]

4 A child accelerates an ice hockey puck of mass 0.16 kg by pushing it with a hockey stick along the ice horizontally. While the child is pushing it, the puck's speed increases from 0 to 15 m/s.

   a Show that the kinetic energy gained by the hockey puck is about 20 J.   [2]

   b State the work done by the child on the hockey puck.
      Include the unit in your answer.   [2]

   c The child pushes the puck with a constant force. While the child is pushing it, the puck moves a distance of 0.40 m. Calculate the force exerted on the puck by the child.   [2]

   d The child pushes the same hockey puck along rough horizontal ground and does the same amount of work as before.

      Predict whether the puck will gain more, less or the same kinetic energy as when it was pushed on ice. Explain your answer.   [3]

                                                           [Total: 9]

> **UNDERSTAND THIS TERM**
> - joule (J)

8.3 Power

1 Machine A does an amount of work W in a time t.
Compare the power of machine A with:

   a machine B, which does the same amount of work, W, over a time that is longer than t

   b machine C, which does more work than W over the same time, t.

2 Which of the following is **not** a correct definition of power?

   A The rate at which work is done.

   B The rate at which a force changes.

   C The rate at which a force does work.

   D The rate at which energy is transferred.

                                                           [Total: 1]

> **UNDERSTAND THIS TERM**
> - power

‹‹ RECALL AND CONNECT 2 ‹‹

Write the steps involved in generating electricity in a coal-fired power station.

8.4 Calculating power

1 **a** How are the units of watts and joules related?

  b The power of an electric hair dryer and the maximum power of a human are both about 2 kW. Write kW as a word. What does it mean?

  c The power of a typical coal power station is about 500 MW. Write MW as a word. What does it mean?

2 Write two equations for efficiency: one in terms of energy and one in terms of power.

3 **a** Define 'power'. [1]

  A helicopter of mass 2500 kg rises vertically at a constant speed, gaining 80 m in height in a time of 50 s.

  b Calculate the work done by the helicopter against gravity. Write your answer in joules. [3]

  c Calculate the power of the helicopter while it is rising at constant speed. Write your answer in watts. [2]

  d State the power of the helicopter in kilowatts. [1]

  e Identify the energy store that the energy is transferred into when the helicopter is moving upwards. [1]

  f The helicopter now accelerates upwards. Predict whether the power of the helicopter will be the same as, greater than or lower than before. Explain your answer. [2]

  [Total: 10]

4 In Qatar at midday on a cloudless day in June, the power of the Sun's radiation falling onto a square metre of horizontal ground is 0.95 kW.

  a Calculate the energy transferred by the Sun's radiation on a square metre of horizontal ground in 1 minute. Write your answer in joules. [3]

  b A photovoltaic cell with area 1.0 m² has efficiency 0.18. Calculate its useful output power if it is used in Qatar at midday on a cloudless day in June. Write your answer in watts. [2]

  c Determine how many of these photovoltaic cells would be needed to give a total useful power output of 1.0 MW. [2]

  [Total: 7]

REFLECTION

In Question 3, three quantities were given before part b, but not all of them were needed to answer part b. How did you decide which quantities to use?

How well are you organising and presenting your written answers to calculation questions? If you looked at your answers in a few days' time, would you still be able to understand them easily?

UNDERSTAND THIS TERM

* watt

SELF-ASSESSMENT CHECKLIST

Let's revisit the Knowledge focus and Exam skills focus for this chapter.

Decide how confident you are with each statement.

Now I can	Show it	Needs more work	Almost there	Confident to move on
learn that work done equals energy transferred, or the force multiplied by the distance moved in the direction of the force	Describe three situations in which work is done. Sketch each of these, showing the force and distance moved.			
calculate work done and power ($W = Fd = \Delta E$ and $P = \Delta E\, t$).	Answer at least one past exam question in which you have to calculate work done.			
relate power to work done and time taken	Recall the definition of power, in words and in symbols.			
show that I understand the command word 'define' and can answer 'define' questions	Write three 'define' questions related to topics that you have already revised.			
identify where I need to improve.	Make a simple plan for how you will do this and discuss it with a classmate.			

Exam practice 2

This section contains past paper questions from previous Cambridge exams, which draws together your knowledge on a range of topics that you have covered up to this point. These questions give you the opportunity to test your knowledge and understanding. Additional past paper practice questions can be found in the accompanying digital material.

The following question has an example student response and commentary provided. Once you have worked through the question, read the student response and commentary. Are your answers different to the sample answers?

1 Figure 1.1 shows the load–extension graphs for two springs, A and B.

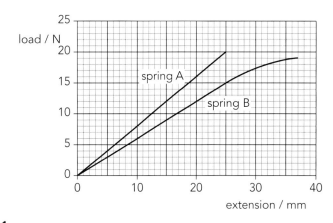

Figure 1.1

a   Determine, in mm, the extension of spring A for a load of 10 N.   [1]

b   State which spring is easier to stretch and give a reason for your answer.   [2]

c   A different spring is suspended from the edge of a bench, as shown in Figure 1.2.

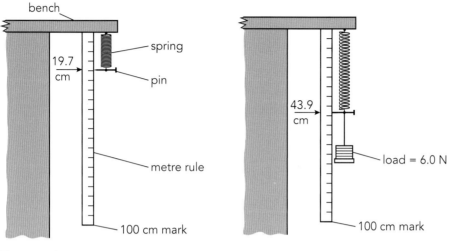

Figure 1.2   **Figure 1.3**

With no load on the spring, the pin points to 19.7 cm on the metre rule, as shown in Figure 1.2.

When a load of 6.0 N is attached to the spring, the pin points to 43.9 cm, as shown in Figure 1.3.

i   Calculate the extension of this spring for a load of 6.0 N.

extension = ... cm.   [1]

ii Describe how a student could use the equipment in Figure 1.2 to obtain accurate readings for a load–extension graph for this spring.   [2]

[Total: 6]

Adapted from *Cambridge IGCSE Physics (0625) Paper 32, Q3, March 2018*

Example student response	Commentary
1 a 8 mm	The student seems to have found the load, 8 (N), that gives an extension of 10 (mm). This is not what the question asks. *This answer is awarded 0 out of 1 mark.*
b A because A stretches in a straight line, while B stretches in a curve.	The student thinks that the graphs show the shape of the stretched springs. They should consider how much force is needed to stretch both springs by the same amount. *This answer is awarded 0 out of 2 marks.*
c i 43.9 – 19.7 = 24.2	This is the correct answer since it is the difference between the stretched length and the unstretched length of the spring. *This answer is awarded 1 out of 1 mark.*

Example student response	Commentary
ii Measure extensions for different loads and plot these on a graph.	The student has written a correct statement summarising the method (although 'plot these on a graph' is not needed). This is enough to gain a mark. However, the student has not added any further detail. They should notice that the question asks how to get *accurate* readings and write one way of trying to achieve this. *This answer is awarded 1 out of 2 marks.*

2 Now that you've gone through the commentary, try to write an improved answer to the parts of the question where you lost marks. This will help you check if you've understood why each mark has (or has not) been allocated. Use the commentary to guide you as you answer.

The following question has an example student response and commentary provided. Once you have read the question, read the student response and commentary.

3 a A force is used to move an object from the Earth's surface to a greater height.

   Explain why the gravitational potential energy (g.p.e.) of the object increases. [1]

   b Figure 3.1 shows a train moving up towards the top of a mountain.

   The train transports 80 passengers, each of average mass 65 kg, through a vertical height of 1600 m.

   Calculate the increase in the total gravitational potential energy (g.p.e.) of the passengers. [2]

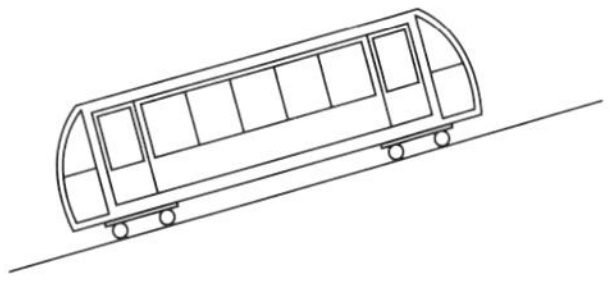

Figure 3.1

   c The engine of the train has a power of 1500 kW. The time taken to reach the top of the mountain is 30 minutes.

   Calculate the efficiency of the engine in raising the 80 passengers 1600 m to the top of the mountain. [4]

[Total: 7]

Cambridge IGCSE Physics (0625), Paper 42, Q2, March 2018

Example student response	Commentary
3 a because the height is greater	This is not enough to gain the mark. The student needs to show how g.p.e. is related to height by writing a formula. *This answer is awarded 0 out of 1 mark.*
b total mass = 80 × 65 = 5200 $mgh = 5200 \times 9.8 \times 1600 \approx 82 \times 10^6$ J	The student has done the correct calculation and has the correct result. They have written their answer in a different way from the mark scheme (which shows the answer in standard form, 8.2×10^7 J), but their answer is equivalent to the correct answer so it still gains the mark. *This answer is awarded 2 out of 2 marks.*

Example student response	Commentary
c $1500\,kW = 1\,500\,000\,W$ $efficiency = \dfrac{useful\ energy\ output}{energy\ input}$ $= \dfrac{82 \times 10^6}{1\,500\,000}$ $= 54\%$	The student has correctly converted kilowatts to watts, but this is not enough to gain a mark. They gain 1 mark for writing the correct equation for efficiency. However, they have used the input power instead of energy input. The mark scheme gives 2 marks for calculating the energy input and 1 mark for the final correct answer, but the student does not gain these marks. *This answer is awarded 1 out of 4 marks.*

4   Now that you've gone through the commentary, try to write a mark scheme for Question **3**. This will help you check if you've understood why each mark has (or has not) been allocated.

The following question has an example student commentary and answer provided. Work through the question first, than compare your answer to the sample answer and commentary. Where were your answers different to the sample answers?

5   Nuclear fission is used in nuclear power stations to release thermal energy.

   a   Describe how the thermal energy is used to generate electricity.   [3]

   b   Describe two environmental problems that are due to using nuclear power stations.   [2]

   [Total: 5]

Cambridge IGCSE Physics (0625) Paper 32, Q6, June 2018

Example student response	Commentary
5 a The thermal energy makes a turbine turn, and the turbine is attached to a generator. A generator is designed to convert kinetic energy to electrical energy when it spins. The electricity is transported by wires, and it is used to power homes, offices and factories.	Thermal energy does not directly turn the turbine – the student has missed two important steps. They have instead focused on energy stores and transfers, and how the electricity is used. This is not what the question asks for. *This answer is awarded 1 out of 3 marks.*
b It makes radioactive waste, which is dangerous. A nuclear power station can explode.	The first point is correct. The second point, although it may be possible, does not state why a nuclear accident would cause an environmental problem. *This answer is awarded 1 out of 2 marks.*

6   Write an improved answer to the parts of the question where you lost marks. It is possible to write a shorter answer to part **a** that gains all three marks, by describing the three key steps in just a few words each.

The following question has an example student commentary and answer provided. Work through the question first, than compare your answer to the sample answer and commentary. Are your answers different to the sample responses? What information does this give you about your understanding of this topic?

7 a i Define *power*. [1]

   ii In the following list, tick the **two** boxes next to the two quantities needed to calculate the work done on an object: [1]

☐ mass of the object

☐ force acting on the object

☐ speed of the object

☐ acceleration of the object

☐ distance moved by the object.

b A lift (elevator) in a high building transports 12 passengers, each of mass 65 kg, through a vertical height of 150 m in a time of 64 s.

   i Calculate the power needed to transport the passengers through this height. [4]

   ii The lift (elevator) is driven by an electric motor.

State a reason, other than friction, why the power supplied by the motor is greater than the power needed to transport the passengers. [1]

[Total: 7]

Cambridge IGCSE Physics (0625) Paper 32, Q3, November 2015

Example student response	Commentary
7 a i the amount of energy transferred in a time	The definition is incomplete. The student has not stated the amount of time. *This answer is awarded 0 out of 1 mark.*
ii ✓ mass of the object ☐ force acting on the object ☐ speed of the object ☐ acceleration of the object ✓ distance moved by the object	The student has chosen one correct quantity and one incorrect quantity. *This answer is awarded 0 out of 1 mark.*
b i 65 × 150 = 9750 9750 ÷ 64 = 152	The student has used the mass of one passenger instead of the total mass of all 12 passengers. They have multiplied mass by distance, which is not the correct way to calculate the work done. The student has attempted to calculate power by dividing (their incorrect) work done by the time taken, which is a correct step. *This answer is awarded 1 out of 4 marks.*

ii	some of the input energy is transferred thermally to internal energy	The question asks for a reason 'other than friction'. The student has described the energy transfer that happens because of friction. They need to write about a different reason why more power is needed. *This answer is awarded 0 out of 1 mark.*

8 Now write an improved answer to the parts of the question where you lost marks, using the commentary to help you. In **b** part **i**, think carefully about how to use the four quantities that are given. You may find it helpful to write them all down (in the form h = 150 m, t = 64 s and so on) and then consider how to use them to calculate the power.

9 The kinetic particle model of matter

In this chapter you will practise answering questions that use the command words 'describe' and 'explain'. It is important that you know the difference between these two command words:

Describe	state the points of a topic/give characteristics and main features.
Explain	set out purposes or reasons/make the relationships between things evident/provide why and/or how and support with relevant evidence.

When you come across questions with two command words make sure you understand what is required for both, and the reasons for different marks available.

9.1 States of matter

1   Fill in the gaps in these statements about changes of state.

   a   The process that occurs when a .... is cooled so that it changes into a liquid, is called ....

   b   The process that occurs when a liquid is cooled so that it changes into a ...., is called .... or ....

   c   When a .... changes into a .... , it changes from being rigid to not being rigid. The process is called ....

   d   When a .... changes into a ...., it changes from having a fixed volume to having no fixed volume. The process is called .... or ....

2   A student has a sample of a liquid and a sample of a gas, in identical sealed (tightly closed) small bottles.

   a   Both of the bottles are full. Compare the masses of the bottles and explain your answer.   [2]

   The student has two identical larger bottles. Each one has twice the volume of one of the smaller bottles. The student transfers each sample to one of the larger bottles and seals it, without losing any of the sample.

   b   Compare the volumes of the liquid and the gas in the two bottles and explain your answer.   [2]

   [Total: 4]

≪ RECALL AND CONNECT 1 ≪

A child pulls a sledge of mass 3.0 kg from the bottom of a slope to the top, by exerting a constant force of 22 N a distance of 25 m along the slope. The top of the hill is 15 m higher than the bottom.

a   Calculate the work done by the child's pulling force.

b   Calculate the gain in gravitational potential energy of the sledge.

c   Calculate the work done by the child's pulling force against the friction acting on the sledge.

UNDERSTAND THESE TERMS

- states of matter
- changes of state
- evaporation
- boiling
- melting
- condensing
- solidifying/ freezing

REFLECTION

When you learn a key term, check that you can recall it two ways. For example, you should be able to give the meaning of the term 'condense' but also recall the term when given its description. Do you remember all of the changes of state in both of these ways? Can you think of mnemonics for any key terms that you find difficult to remember?

9.2 The kinetic particle model of matter

1 a Produce sketches showing the particles in a gas, liquid and solid. Your sketches should clearly show any differences between the arrangements and separations of the particles.

   b How does the motion of the particles differ in gases, liquids and solids?

2 a What happens to the motion of microscopic particles as the temperature increases?

   b What is the only temperature, in degrees Celsius, at which the particles in matter have no kinetic energy?

   c What is the name of this temperature?

3 a In the 'kinetic particle model of matter', what does the word 'particle' refer to?

   b In which state of matter are the forces between particles:

   i strongest

   ii weakest?

4 a Compare:

   i the arrangements of particles in solids and liquids [1]

   ii the average separations of particles in liquids and gases [1]

   iii the motions of particles in solids and liquids. [1]

   b Brownian motion can be seen by using a microscope to observe grains of dust in water.

   Describe and explain the observations. [4]

   c A student wants to find out whether Brownian motion can happen in a solid. They make a lump of glass with some dust grains inside it. They observe the dust grains under a microscope.

   Predict and explain the observations. [2]

   [Total: 9]

5 a Use the kinetic particle model of matter to explain:

   i why gases can be compressed [2]

   ii why liquids can be poured [2]

   iii why solids have a fixed shape. [2]

   b Explain why scientists use models. [1]

   [Total: 7]

UNDERSTAND
THESE TERMS

- absolute zero
- attractive force
- atom
- bonds
- Brownian motion
- kinetic particle model of matter
- molecule
- model
- observations

9.3 Gases and the kinetic model

1 a   Why does a gas exert a pressure on the walls of its container?

   b   How would you calculate the force on a rectangular wall of a container of gas, given the length and width of the wall and the pressure of the gas?

2   A student has a syringe containing air, as shown in Figure 9.1. The syringe is sealed so that the air cannot escape.

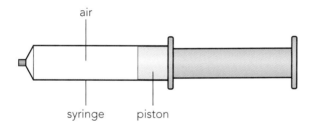

Figure 9.1

The student pushes the piston to the left. During this process, the temperature of the air inside the syringe does not change.

a   State and explain what happens to the force the student needs to exert as the piston moves further to the left.   [3]

b   Explain why the pressure exerted by a gas on its container increases when the temperature of the gas increases.   [2]

[Total: 5]

9.4 Temperature and the Celsius scale

1   For each statement below, decide whether it is describing temperature or internal energy.

    a   This quantity does not depend on the size of the object.

    b   This quantity is measured in joules.

    c   This quantity is a measure of the average kinetic energy of the particles in an object.

    d   This quantity is the total energy of all the particles in an object.

    e   This quantity can be measured in Kelvin.

    f   This quantity is a measure of how cold or hot an object is.

2   a   What is the lowest possible temperature in Kelvin?

    b   What are the symbols used for temperature in degrees Celsius and temperature in Kelvin?

    c   How can you convert a temperature from degrees Celsius to Kelvin, and how can you convert from Kelvin to degrees Celsius?

3   a   Describe what happens to the motion of particles in a solid as the temperature of the solid decreases.   [1]

    b   Explain why there is a lowest possible temperature.   [1]

[Total: 2]

4   The greatest temperature change in one location in 24 hours was in 1972 in a location in Montana, USA. The temperature at 9 a.m. was −48°C.

    a   Calculate the temperature in Kelvin.   [1]

The temperature at 8 a.m. the next morning was 282 K.

    b   Calculate this temperature in degrees Celsius.   [1]

    c   Determine the increase in temperature in degrees Celsius.   [1]

    d   Explain why the change in temperature has the same value in Kelvin as it has in degrees Celsius.   [1]

[Total: 4]

> UNDERSTAND THESE TERMS
> - calibrate
> - fixed points
> - Kelvin temperature scale
> - temperature

≪ RECALL AND CONNECT 2 ≪

A tractor moves a distance 100 m in a straight line by exerting a constant force of 16 000 N for a time of 16 s.

Calculate the power of the tractor.

9.5 The gas laws

1   Write the relationship between the pressure and volume of a fixed mass of gas
    at constant temperature in each of the following ways:

    a   by expressing what is constant for the gas

    b   using the symbol $\propto$ (is proportional to)

    c   by relating the pressure and volume before a change is made to the pressure
    and volume after the change.

2   A student carries out an experiment to investigate the relationship between
    pressure and volume of a constant mass of gas.

    a   State one *other* variable that should be kept constant during
    the experiment.   [1]

The student can increase the pressure of the gas using a pump.

They use a pressure gauge to measure the pressure of the gas inside a glass tube.
A scale next to the tube shows the volume of gas inside the tube.

The apparatus is shown in Figure 9.2.

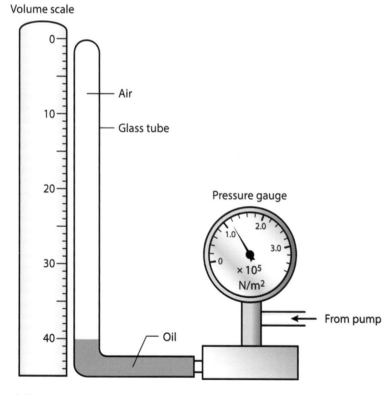

Figure 9.2

b The pressure of the gas is 1.14×10^5 Pa when its volume is 40 cm³. Predict the pressure of the gas when its volume is 30 cm³. [2]

c When the pressure gauges shows a reading of 2.28×10^5 Pa, the student measures a gas volume of 24 cm³. Comment on this result. [1]

d The student draws a graph of their results, with p on the y-axis and $\frac{1}{V}$ on the x-axis. Figure 9.3 shows the shape of the student's line of best fit.

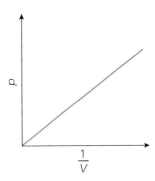

Figure 9.3

i Describe the relationship between p and $\frac{1}{V}$. [1]

ii Sketch the shape of the graph of p against V. [1]

[Total: 6]

SELF-ASSESSMENT CHECKLIST

Let's revisit the Knowledge focus and Exam skills focus for this chapter.

Decide how confident you are with each statement.

Now I can	Show it	Needs more work	Almost there	Confident to move on
describe the three states of matter (solid, liquid and gas)	Make a table summarising the properties of the three states.			
investigate changes of state	Describe the visible changes that occur when a substance melts or boils.			
use the kinetic model to explain changes of state and the behaviour of gases	Create a poster or cartoon explaining changes of state, why gases have pressure and why the pressure of a gas changes when its temperature or volume changes.			

CONTINUED

Now I can	Show it	Needs more work	Almost there	Confident to move on
explain the kinetic particle model in terms of the forces between particles	Explain, in terms of forces between particles, why gases fill their container.			
calculate changes in the pressure and volume of a gas	Answer at least one exam-style question or past exam question about the gas laws.			
show that I understand the command words 'describe' and 'explain' and can answer 'describe' and 'explain' questions.	Say what 'describe' and 'explain' means. Write an exam-style question that includes both command words and create a mark scheme for it.			

10 Thermal properties of matter

KNOWLEDGE FOCUS

In this chapter, you will answer questions on:

- thermal expansion

> specific heat capacity

- changing state.

EXAM SKILLS FOCUS

In this chapter you will:

- develop the habit of reading questions thoroughly.

During an exam, it can be tempting to read questions very quickly, or even not to read some of the information given, because you are under time pressure. However, if this causes you to misread the command word, miss a key piece of information or misunderstand the question, you may write an inappropriate or incorrect answer, or be unable to answer at all.

If you get into the habit of reading questions thoroughly during your revision, you will be more likely to do this during the exams. You may find the following strategies helpful: read the question twice, especially if a lot of information is given; try to visualise or imagine what the information is telling you; and make a conscious effort to read any text that appears above, below or within a diagram, instead of only looking at the diagram.

10.1 Thermal expansion

1   Write one or two sentences to describe:

    a   a use of the thermal expansion of a solid

    b   a use of the thermal expansion of a liquid

    c   a problem that can be caused by thermal expansion, and a way of preventing it.

2   Table 10.1 shows how much a 10 cm long piece of each solid expands when its temperature rises by 10°C.

Material	Expansion / mm
aluminium	0.03
concrete	0.01
glass	0.003
steel	0.01

Table 10.1

a   A glass jar has a lid made of steel. Using information from Table 10.1, explain why is easier to unscrew the lid if you run hot water over the lid for a few seconds.   [1]

b   A strip of aluminium and a strip of steel are joined firmly together to make a bimetallic strip.

    When the bimetallic strip is heated, it bends as shown in Figure 10.1.

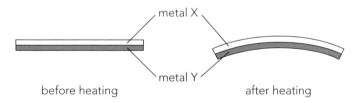

before heating   after heating

Figure 10.1

Use information from Table 10.1 to deduce which metal, X or Y, is aluminium. Explain your answer.   [2]

c   Concrete is used as a building material. It can be made stronger by having metal bars inside it. The bars are usually made of steel.

    Using information from Table 10.1, suggest and explain what might go wrong if aluminium bars were used instead.   [2]

[Total: 5]

UNDERSTAND THIS TERM

- thermal expansion

10.2 Specific heat capacity

1   a   For each of the symbols c, E, m and θ in the formula $c = \dfrac{\Delta E}{m \Delta \theta}$, name the quantity and write a unit that can be used for each quantity.

   b   In the equation $c = \dfrac{\Delta E}{m \Delta \theta}$, what is the meaning of the symbol Δ?

   c   What is the meaning of the statement: 'the specific heat capacity of ice is 2100 J/(kg °C)'?

2   a   Define the specific heat capacity of a substance. [2]

   b   A student carries out an experiment to measure the specific heat capacity of water. The apparatus is set up as shown below.

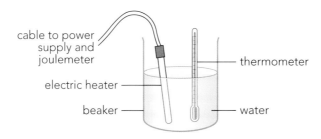

cable to power supply and joulemeter
electric heater
beaker
thermometer
water

Figure 10.2

The initial temperature of the water is the temperature of the room, which is 22.0°C.

The student obtains the following measurements:

   mass of water = 0.800 kg

   energy supplied to water = 115 000 J

   initial temperature of water = 22.0°C

   final temperature of water = 49.7°C.

Use the measurements to calculate the specific heat capacity of water. Include the unit in your answer. [4]

c The student repeats the experiment but this time the temperature of the water starts 10°C below room temperature and finishes 10°C above room temperature. The measured specific heat capacity this time is more accurate. Suggest why. [1]

d Suggest and explain **two** other ways to improve the experiment to give as accurate a result as possible. [4]

[Total: 11]

3 In cold weather, some people use a hot water bottle to warm their bed at night. This is a sealed rubber bottle with hot water inside it.

A hot water bottle contains 1.4 kg of water. The temperature of the water is 38°C. The specific heat capacity of water is 4200 J/(kg °C).

a Calculate the temperature of the water after 110 000 J of energy has been transferred from the water to the surroundings. [3]

An identical bottle is now filled with 1.4 kg of liquid X at 38°C. Liquid X has a much lower specific heat capacity than water.

b Suggest why the bottle of liquid X cools more quickly than the bottle of water. [1]

[Total: 4]

> **UNDERSTAND THIS TERM**
>
> • specific heat capacity

10.3 Changing state

1 A sample of a substance is supplied with heat at a constant rate.
The graph shows how the temperature of the sample changes with time.

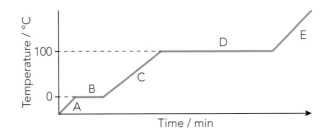

Figure 10.3: A temperature against time graph for a substance that is being heated

a For each of the sections labelled A to E, write down:
  i the effect that the energy input has on the sample
  ii which state(s) the sample is in
  iii which change of state is happening, if any.

2 a Give **three** differences between boiling and evaporation.

  b List **three** factors that increase the rate of evaporation of a liquid.

3   A sealed container of a pure substance is placed inside a freezer.
    The graph shows how the temperature of the substance changes with time.

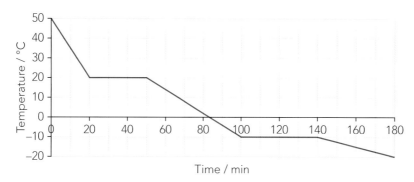

Figure 10.4

a   Using Figure 10.4, deduce the boiling temperature of the substance.   [1]
b   Give the state(s) of matter of the substance at:
    i   40°C   [1]
    ii   12°C.   [1]
c   Predict the state of the substance at 70°C.   [1]
d   State what is happening to separations of the particles of the substance
    at 30 minutes.   [1]
e   Between 100 and 140 minutes, thermal energy is given out by the
    substance but its temperature does not decrease. Explain why.   [2]

                                                                    [Total: 7]

4   A student carries out an experiment to compare the evaporation of water and alcohol.

    She takes two identical thermometers, A and B, both at room temperature.

    She wraps the bulb of A in cotton wool soaked in water.

    She wraps the bulb of B in cotton wool soaked in alcohol.

    She clamps both thermometers as shown below, taking care not to leave either
    of them in a draught (moving air).

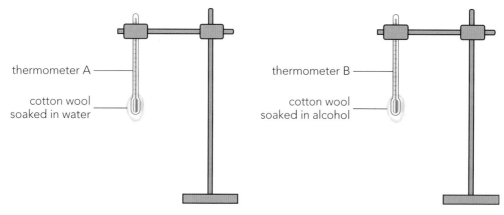

Figure 10.5

After 2 minutes, she takes the reading on each thermometer.
The results are shown in the table.

Thermometer	Reading on thermometer at start / °C	Reading on thermometer after 2 minutes / °C
A (water)	21.0	19.5
B (alcohol)	21.0	15.5

a   Determine the temperature change of thermometer B. [1]

b   Suggest why the student takes care not to leave the thermometers in a draught. [1]

c   Explain why a liquid cools while it is evaporating. [2]

d   Alcohol has a lower boiling point than water. Use this fact to explain the difference between the temperature changes of thermometers A and B. [1]

[Total: 5]

UNDERSTAND THESE TERMS

• boiling point
• melting point

REFLECTION

There was a lot of information to read at the beginning of Question 4. Did you take care to read the information thoroughly before you started answering the question? When the question describes an experiment, one way to make sure you have taken in the information correctly is to imagine yourself carrying out the steps described. Would this be a helpful technique for you?

SELF-ASSESSMENT CHECKLIST

Let's revisit the Knowledge focus and Exam skills focus for this chapter.

Decide how confident you are with each statement.

Now I can	Show it	Needs more work	Almost there	Confident to move on
describe how and why solids, liquids and gases expand when their temperatures rise	Create a comic strip, slideshow or animation to show what happens to the particles during expansion of a solid, liquid and gas.			
measure the specific heat capacity of some materials	Carry out an experiment to measure the specific heat capacity of a material. Write a report on your experiment.			

CONTINUED

Now I can	Show it	Needs more work	Almost there	Confident to move on
explain some everyday uses and consequences of thermal expansion	Share ideas with a classmate, taking it in turns to describe and explain one use or consequence.			
relate energy supplied to increase in temperature when an object is heated	Sketch a graph of temperature against time as a pure substance cools, starting as a gas and then condensing and solidifying. Describe what is happening in each section of your graph.			
explain changes of state using the kinetic model of matter	Plan how you would explain this to a student who is a year or two younger than you.			
develop the habit of reading questions thoroughly.	Do a few past exam questions, or a whole paper, paying attention to reading the questions carefully. If you get an answer wrong because you misread the question, try to identify what you misread and how that affected your answer.			

11 Thermal energy transfers

KNOWLEDGE FOCUS

In this chapter, you will answer questions on:

- conduction
- convection
- radiation
- consequences of thermal energy transfer.

EXAM SKILLS FOCUS

In this chapter you will:

- show that you understand the 'comment' command word, and can answer 'comment' questions.

In this chapter you will practise answering questions that use the command word 'comment'. It is important that you are able to recognise how to answer questions using this command word and know what it is instructing you to do:

| Comment | give an informed opinion. |

This command word usually appears in questions about experiments, where you are asked your opinion about part of the method or result. Your opinion should be informed by your knowledge of physics and your experience of performing experiments.

11.1 Conduction

1 Copy and complete the sentences using the words below. You may need to use each word twice, once, or not at all.

| conductor | insulator | good | bad | quickly | slowly |

A substance that conducts thermal energy very slowly is called a thermal
....

A substance that conducts thermal energy quickly is called a thermal ....

A .... insulator is a poor ....

If you touch a thermal insulator and a thermal conductor that are at the same temperature, the thermal .... feels colder because it conducts thermal energy away from your hand more ....

2 A student carries out an experiment to investigate the transfer of thermal energy along a rod, using the apparatus shown in Figure 11.1.

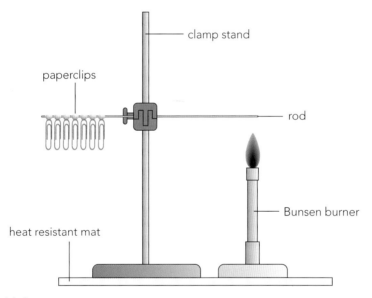

clamp stand

paperclips

rod

Bunsen burner

heat resistant mat

Figure 11.1

Each paperclip is attached to the rod using a small amount of wax, which has a low melting point. A paperclip falls if the wax attaching it to the rod melts.

a   The rod is a good thermal conductor. Suggest a suitable material for the rod. [1]

b   Predict and explain which paperclip will fall first. [2]

c   Another student does this experiment using a glass rod. Comment on the student's choice of rod material. [2]

[Total: 5]

3 a   Explain, using the idea of particles, how thermal conduction occurs in a glass rod that is heated at one end. [3]

b   Metals are good thermal conductors because they contain particles that can move freely, transferring energy quickly from one part of the metal to another. Give the name of these particles. [1]

c   Explain, in terms of particles, why thermal conduction happens very slowly in gases. [1]

[Total: 5]

UNDERSTAND THESE TERMS

- thermal conduction
- thermal conductor
- thermal insulator
- electron

REFLECTION

Were you confident about how to answer Question 2c which included the command word 'comment'? If you got the answer wrong, check the meaning of this command word and try to understand why.

11.2 Convection

1 Give two ways in which convection can be useful in the home.

2 In many countries, homes use heating during cold weather.

a   Explain why the air above a heater rises. [3]

In many countries, homes use air conditioning during hot weather. An air conditioning unit cools a room by blowing out cold air.

b   Explain why the unit will not be very effective at cooling a room if it is located near the floor. [2]

[Total: 5]

3   A student wants to test whether water is a good thermal conductor.
They trap a piece of ice at the bottom of a boiling tube of water.
They hold the top of the tube near a flame, as shown in Figure 11.2.

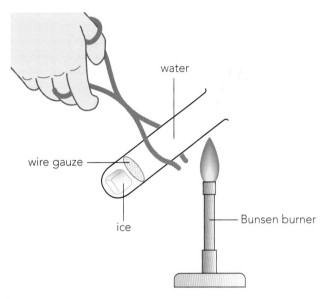

Figure 11.2

a   When the water at the top of the tube boils, the ice cube is still frozen.
Explain how this is possible.   [2]

b   The student chose from two materials to hold the ice at the bottom of the
tube: wire gauze (made of a grid of metal wires) or sand. Either of these
materials could trap the ice effectively. Comment on the student's choice
of wire gauze.   [2]

Another student wants to try the experiment but does not have any wire gauze.
This student lets the ice cube float at the top of the water and holds the
bottom of the tube near the flame. The ice cube melts quickly.

c   Explain why this happens.   [2]

[Total: 6]

> **UNDERSTAND THESE TERMS**
> - convection
> - convection current
> - density
> - fluid

11.3 Radiation

1   Decide whether each of the following statements is true or false.

a   Infrared radiation is a form of electromagnetic radiation.

b   Infrared radiation can be detected by the skin.

c   If an object's temperature is below 0°C, it does not emit infrared radiation.

d   Shiny and light-coloured objects are good emitters and poor absorbers
of infrared radiation.

e   Matte black objects are poor reflectors of infrared radiation.

2   When the air around a person is at a lower temperature than their body, the person loses heat. Table 11.1 shows typical percentages of heat lost in different ways.

Method(s) of heat loss	Percentage of total / %
radiation	60
evaporation	25
conduction and convection	15

Table 11.1

a   When people do physical activity in extremely cold temperatures, they often try not to work hard enough to cause sweating. Use information from the table to explain why.   [1]

b   When a person is rescued in cold weather, it is important to keep them warm. Rescuers often wrap the person in a thin foil sheet, called an emergency blanket.

   i   An emergency blanket is more effective than a normal blanket (such as a blanket made of wool), even though a normal blanket is a better insulator. Use information from the table to explain why.   [2]

   ii   An emergency blanket often has one side that is shiny and one side that is matte. State and explain which side should be on the inside (next to the person's body).   [2]

[Total: 5]

3   An animal is sitting on a rock. Its life processes cause a transfer of energy from its chemical store to its thermal store at a rate of 0.1 W. Thermal energy transfers into the animal from its surroundings at a rate of 0.4 W.

At the same time, thermal energy transfers out of the animal at a rate of 0.8 W.

a   State and explain whether the temperature of the animal is increasing, decreasing, or constant. Include a calculation in your answer.   [3]

Some types of lizards can make their skin become darker if they want to increase their temperature on a hot, sunny day.

b   Explain why this is helpful to the lizard.   [1]

c   Suggest why this might not be a helpful strategy on a cold, cloudy day.   [2]

[Total: 6]

> **UNDERSTAND THIS TERM**
>
> • infrared radiation

≪ RECALL AND CONNECT ≪

Some trains have tyres that are made of steel. A tyre is heated to a high temperature and fitted onto the wheel of a train while it is hot. Why is this done?

11.4 Consequences of thermal energy transfer

1 Describe three ways of slowing thermal energy transfer between a room and its surroundings. For each one, name the main method(s) of thermal transfer that is/are reduced.

2 Figure 11.3 shows a vacuum flask. It can be used to keep a hot drink hot for many hours.

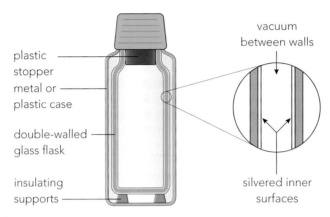

Figure 11.3

a Give **two** reasons why the rate of thermal energy transfer through the flask by conduction is very low. [2]

b Give **one** feature of the flask that is designed to reduce thermal energy transfer by radiation and explain how it works. [2]

c The same flask can also be used to keep a cold drink cold for many hours. Explain why. [1]

[Total: 5]

3 When a car engine is running, energy is transferred to its internal energy store. To prevent the engine from overheating, the car has a cooling system made up of metal pipes through which a liquid (usually water) flows, as shown in Figure 11.4.

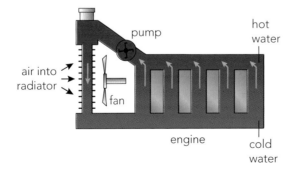

Figure 11.4

a State a property of water that makes it effective at carrying away a lot of thermal energy. Explain why. [2]

b Identify the main method of thermal energy transfer from:

  i the engine into the cooling system [1]

  ii the bottom of the cooling system to the top of the cooling system. [1]

The radiator, at the left side in Figure 11.4, is designed to transfer thermal energy quickly to the surrounding air.

c The outside of a car radiator is often painted black. Explain why. [2]

d The radiator contains a lot of gaps through which air can move. Suggest a reason why the fan switches on when the engine is hot. [1]

[Total: 7]

SELF-ASSESSMENT CHECKLIST

Let's revisit the Knowledge focus and Exam skills focus for this chapter.

Decide how confident you are with each statement.

Now I can	Show it	Needs more work	Almost there	Confident to move on
carry out experiments to demonstrate conduction, convection and radiation	For each type of thermal energy transfer, carry out an experiment. Write a report, including: the method, results or observations, a conclusion (which interprets your results) and an evaluation of your method, including possible improvements.			
explain why some materials conduct and others do not	Plan how you would explain, to a classmate who missed the lessons on conduction, how conduction occurs in non-metals and metals.			
describe and explain convection currents	Draw a picture showing a situation in which there is a convection current. Draw arrows to show convection and add labels to describe and explain what is happening at different places.			
explain thermal energy radiation	Create a summary or mind map showing what you know about thermal energy radiation, including at least six pieces of information.			

CONTINUED

Now I can	Show it	Needs more work	Almost there	Confident to move on
investigate the differences between good and bad emitters of radiation	Carry out an experiment to investigate good and bad emitters. Explain your results and evaluate your method.			
research applications and consequences of thermal energy transfer	In a group of three or four classmates, each research one application or consequence, and then teach each other about what you have discovered.			
show that I understand the 'comment' command word, and can answer 'comment' questions.	Check whether you gained full marks in the two 'comment' questions in this chapter. If not, read again the definition at the beginning of this chapter and make sure you understand what it means.			

12 Sound

In this chapter you will encounter many of the command words that you have previously practised. When you read an Exam skills question, pay particular attention to the command word and think about what it is asking you to do. If you need to remind yourself what a command word means, you can find all of the command words and their definitions in the IGCSE Physics exam specification.

Several of the more complex exam questions rely on using multiple command words in the question such as 'describe' and 'explain' or 'suggest' and 'explain'. This type of question usually carries higher marks, with full marks only being awarded when both command words are covered in the answer. There are a number of these questions in this chapter so make sure when you answer them that you ensure you cover both command words in your answers to be able to get the full marks available.

12.1 Making sound

1 Complete the sentences by selecting the correct words from the list.

| vibrations | percussion | stringed | wind | length | body |

Musical instruments create .... that we can then hear as sound.
.... instruments, such as guitars, are plucked to make the strings vibrate.
The notes played can be varied by changing the .... of the strings.
.... instruments, such as the drums, create sound when their skins
vibrate. The sound is amplified by the hollow .... of the instrument.
.... instruments, such as the flute, create sound when the column
of air inside them vibrates.

2 How is sound produced when humans speak?

3 Give an example of a musical instrument for each of the following categories
and identify the part of each instrument that vibrates to make the sound.

Type of instrument	Example of instrument	Part that vibrates to create the sound
Percussion		
Stringed		
Wind		

[Total: 6]

≪ RECALL AND CONNECT 1 ≪

State three ways thermal energy can transfer from one place to another. Which
of these does not require a medium to travel through?

12.2 How does sound travel?

1 How does sound travel through a material?

2 On 26 October 2017, NASA put together a compilation of the elusive 'sounds'
of howling planets and whistling helium for Halloween on their website.
Why can we see the planets from Earth but not hear the sounds they make?

3   The tuning fork was invented by the British musician, John Shore in 1711 as a pitch standard used to tune musical instruments. Over time, it has found many other uses.

   a   Figure 12.1 shows a vibrating tuning fork. Sketch the sound waves produced by the fork. You should label areas of compression and rarefaction.   [2]

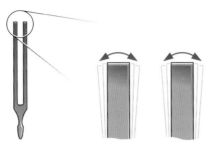

Figure 12.1

   b   A student hits the tuning fork so that it vibrates, and holds its handle against a table. Then the student presses one ear to the table and hears the sound. A teacher who is standing next to the table also hears the sound. Predict who will hear the sound first, and explain your answer.   [2]

[Total: 4]

> **UNDERSTAND THESE TERMS**
> - compression
> - rarefaction

≪ RECALL AND CONNECT 2 ≪

Explain, using the idea of density, how convection happens in a cold room after a heater is switched on.

12.3. The speed of sound

≪ RECALL AND CONNECT 3 ≪

An aircraft travels 1500 m in 5 s. What is its speed?

1   A student hears thunder 12 s after they see the lightning. Calculate the approximate distance between the student and the storm.

2   A student connects two microphones to an electronic timer. The student bangs together two wooden blocks next to one of the microphones. The timer starts when it receives a signal from the microphone next to the blocks. The timer stops when it receives a signal from the other microphone.

   a   Describe how the students can use a measurement from the timer, together with one other measurement, to determine the speed of sound.   [2]

   b   Calculate the speed of sound if the time measurement was 2 ms and the distance between the two microphones was 6 m.   [3]

[Total: 5]

3   In a baseball game the pitcher throws a ball to the batter, who is standing at a distance of 20 m away. Calculate the time it will take for the sound of the bat hitting the ball to reach the pitcher if the speed of sound in air is 340 m/s. **[Total: 2]**

4   Student 'X' is standing at a distance of 30 m from the face of a cliff and blows a whistle. Student 'Y' stands next to 'X' and measures the time taken for the echo of the sound to reach him as 200 ms. Use these values to calculate the speed of sound in air. **[Total: 4]**

5   A scientist makes the statement: 'The speed of sound in air at 40°C is 355 m/s and at –10°C it is 325 m/s.' Suggest the relationship between speed of sound and temperature. **[Total: 1]**

12.4 Seeing and hearing sounds

1   A cathode ray oscilloscope is connected to a microphone. A teacher brings a vibrating tuning fork with a frequency of 200 Hz close to the microphone and the oscilloscope displays a representation of the sound wave as shown in Figure 12.2.

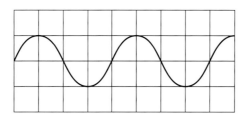

Figure 12.2: Representation of sound wave in an oscilloscope

a   How is the waveform seen on the oscilloscope screen produced?

b   The teacher replaces the tuning fork with a tuning fork of 100 Hz. How will this change the representation of the sound wave on the oscilloscope screen in Figure 12.2?

c   The teacher bangs the tuning fork harder than before to make a louder sound. How will this change the representation of the sound wave on the oscilloscope screen?

d   Choose the correct words to complete the following sentences.

Increasing the frequency affects the (amplitude/pitch/speed) of the sound. Increasing the volume affects the (amplitude/pitch/wavelength/speed) of the sound.

2 The greater wax moth is capable of sensing sounds with frequencies up to 300 kHz.

    a Can a human hear a frequency of 300 kHz? Why or why not?

    b A bat sends out high frequency sound waves and receives an echo
       from a moth after 5.0 ms. The speed of sound in air is 330 m/s.
       What is the distance between the bat and the moth?

3 An oscilloscope is set at 50 ms/div, which means each horizontal division on the
grid represents 30 ms. A microphone is connected to the oscilloscope and it detects
a sound. The oscilloscope screen is shown in Figure 12.3.

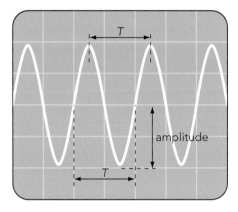

Figure 12.3

    a Determine the frequency of the wave. [2]

    b The volume of the sound increases. Predict the change in the waveform. [1]

    c Figure 12.4 shows four sound waves observed on an oscilloscope.
       The vertical and horizontal scales used are the same every time.

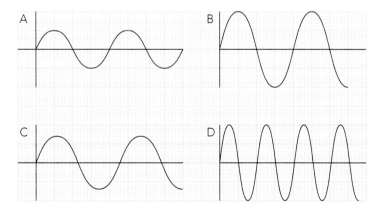

Figure 12.4

    i Compare the volumes of sounds B and D. Explain your answer. [2]

    ii State which wave has the highest pitch. Explain your answer. [2]

    iii State which two waves represent sounds with the same pitch. [1]

[Total: 8]

UNDERSTAND THESE TERMS
• amplitude
• frequency
• hertz

4 A ship in the Baltic Sea uses sonar to measure the depth of the water.
It sends out an ultrasonic wave which bounces back from the seabed after 5.0 s.

   a Calculate the depth of the water. Assume the speed of sound in water
to be 1500 m/s.   [3]

   b The ship travels to the Pacific Ocean where the water is much saltier,
and notices that at the same depth and temperature, the time taken for
the sound to bounce back is 4.9 s. Calculate the speed of the sound.   [2]

   c Deduce how the saltiness of the water affects the speed of sound.   [1]

   d Explain how ultrasonic waves are used to make images of a fetus
in the womb.   [2]

[Total: 8]

REFLECTION

Did you try all of the Exam skills questions in this chapter and check your
answers? If any of your answers are incorrect, one possible reason is that you
misread or misunderstood one or more command words. Where you got an
answer wrong, read the question again to check why.

SELF-ASSESSMENT CHECKLIST

Let's revisit the Knowledge focus and Exam skills focus for this chapter.

Decide how confident you are with each statement.

Now I can	Show it	Needs more work	Almost there	Confident to move on
describe how sounds are produced and how they travel	Draw and explain longitudinal waves with areas of compression and rarefaction.			
measure the speed of sound	Calculate the speed of sound in numerical problems using key equations.			
describe how the amplitude and frequency of a sound wave are linked to its loudness and pitch	Draw waveforms to show how varying loudness of sound impacts the amplitude of waves. Compare waveforms to determine amplitude and frequency.			

CONTINUED

Now I can	Show it	Needs more work	Almost there	Confident to move on
state the range of human hearing	Categorize frequencies of sound as infrasonic, sonic and ultrasonic.			
define the term 'ultrasound' and describe some of its applications	Explain the use of ultrasound to detect flaws inside materials and its use in medicine. Solve numerical problem to determine speed of sound in SONAR navigation. Explain how SONAR navigation uses ultrasonic waves to locate objects under water.			
practise answering questions with a variety of command words.	Find the command words in each question part of the Exam skills questions in this chapter and say why you think those particular command words were used.			

Exam practice 3

This section contains past paper questions from previous Cambridge exams, which draws together your knowledge on a range of topics that you have covered up to this point. These questions give you the opportunity to test your knowledge and understanding. Additional past paper practice questions can be found in the accompanying digital material.

The following question has an example student response and commentary provided. Once you have worked through the question, read the student response and commentary. Are your answers different to the sample answers?

1 A rigid container is filled with a gas.

    a Describe the movement and arrangement of the gas molecules in the container. [3]

    b The gas in the container is heated. The volume of the gas does **not** change.

       State and explain the change in pressure of the gas as the temperature of the gas increases. Use your ideas about molecules in your answer. [3]

[Total: 6]

Cambridge IGCSE Physics (0625) Paper 32, Q4, November 2020

Example student response	Commentary
1 a They move quickly from place to place.	1 mark is gained for mentioning that the molecules move at high speed.
	The student has not mentioned that the movement is random and has not written anything about the arrangement of the particles (which is random, with large separations between the molecules).
	This answer is awarded 1 out of 3 marks.
b The particles move faster when the gas gets hotter, so they collide more with the container walls.	The student has not responded to the 'state' command word, which is worth 1 mark.
	The student has correctly mentioned that the particles move faster, which gains 1 mark. However, 'collide more' does not gain a mark because it does not express the idea clearly enough. The particles collide 'more often' or 'more frequently' with the walls. (The student could also have mentioned that the collisions exert a greater force.)
	This answer is awarded 1 out of 3 marks.

2   Now you have read the commentary to the previous question, here is a question on a similar topic which you should attempt. Use the information from the previous response and commentary to guide you as you answer.

3   a   Table 3.1 gives a list of statements about molecules in gases and solids.

    Put **one** tick in every row to indicate whether each statement refers to a gas or a solid.   [4]

statement	gas	solid
molecules are closely packed		
molecules are free to move around from place to place		
molecules are far apart compared to their size		
molecules can only vibrate about a fixed position		
molecules change position randomly		

Table 3.1

b   Figure 3.1 represents a smoke particle in air. The smoke particle is moving.

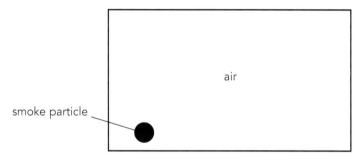

Figure 3.1

Figure 3.2 shows the path of the smoke particle and the position of the smoke particle a short time later.

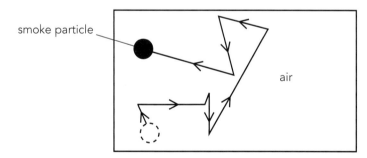

Figure 3.2

i   State the term given to the movement of the smoke particle.   [1]

ii   State what the motion of the smoke particle shows about air molecules.   [3]

[Total: 8]

Cambridge IGCSE Physics (0625) Paper 32, Q6, March 2020

The following question has an example student response and commentary provided.
Once you have completed the question, read the student response and commentary.
Are your answers different to the sample answers?

4 An electrical heater is placed on the floor of a room in a house.
The heater is switched on.

a State the main process by which thermal energy is transferred
to the air in all parts of the room. [1]

b The heater has a power of 1.5 kW. The air in the room has a mass
of 65 kg. The specific heat capacity of air is 720 J / (kg °C).

i Calculate the time it takes for this heater to raise the temperature
of the air in the room from 8.0 °C to 15.0 °C. [4]

ii State **two** reasons why the time calculated in **b i** is smaller
than the actual time taken to raise the temperature of the air
in the room from 8.0 °C to 15.0 °C. [2]

[**Total: 7**]

Cambridge IGCSE Physics (0625) Paper 42, Q6, March 2019

Example student response	Commentary
4 a convection	This is the correct choice out of the three methods of thermal energy transfer (conduction, convection and radiation). *This answer is awarded 1 out of 1 mark.*
b i $\Delta\theta = 15.0 - 8.0 = 7.0°C$ $\Delta E = mc\Delta\theta$ $\quad = 65 \times 720 \times 7.0$ $\quad = 327\,600 \text{ J}$ $t = \dfrac{P}{\Delta E}$ $\quad = \dfrac{1500}{327\,600}$ $\quad = 4.58 \times 10^{-3}\,\text{s}$	The student has set out their calculations very clearly, showing all of the steps. They have made one error: rearranging $P = \dfrac{\Delta E}{t}$ incorrectly to get $t = \dfrac{P}{\Delta E}$. The student has failed to notice that their answer, a few thousandths of a second, is unrealistically short for the time to heat a room. The student gains 1 mark for correctly stating the specific heat capacity equation and 1 mark for correctly calculating the specific heat capacity. *This answer is awarded 2 out of 4 marks.*
ii The walls and furniture get heated up as well as the air. There is more than 65 kg of air in the room.	The student's first statement is correct (since some of the thermal energy from the heater goes into the walls and furniture and therefore there is less available for heating the air). The student's second statement suggests that information given in the question is incorrect. In a question like this, students are expected to assume that the information given is correct and use their understanding of physics to think of other possible explanations. *This answer is awarded 1 out of 2 marks*

Now that you've gone through the commentary, have a go at writing a full mark
scheme for Question 4. This will check that you've understood exactly why each mark
has (or has not) been allocated.

Here is a similar question which you should attempt. Use the information from the previous response and commentary to guide you as you answer. Take care to set out the calculation clearly.

5 a i A liquid is heated so that bubbles of its vapour rise to the surface and molecules escape to the atmosphere.

State the name of this process. [1]

ii At a lower temperature than in **a i**, molecules escape from the surface to the atmosphere.

State the name of this process. [1]

b i Figure 4.1 shows apparatus used to determine the power output of a heater.

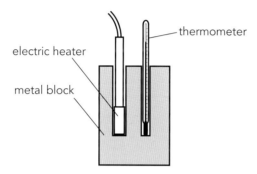

Figure 5.1

The metal block has a mass of 2.7 kg. The metal of the block has a specific heat capacity of 900 J/(kg °C).

In 2 min 30 s, the temperature of the block increases from 21 °C to 39 °C.

Calculate the power of the heater. [4]

ii State and explain a precaution that can be taken to improve the accuracy of the experiment. [2]

[Total: 8]

Cambridge IGCSE Physics (0625) Paper 42, Q5, June 2019

The following question has an example student commentary and answer provided. Work through the question first, then compare your answer to the sample answer and commentary. Where were your answers different to the sample answers?

6   Figure 6.1 shows an electrical heater placed so that it is the same distance from two cans.

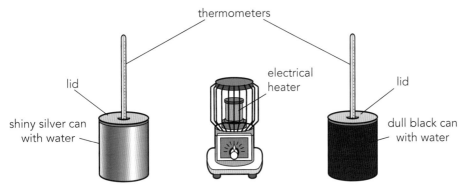

Figure 6.1

The cans are the same size and contain equal volumes of water, initially at the same temperature.

a   Energy travels to the cans from the heater.

State the name of this process.   [1]

b   Both cans are heated by the process in **a** for 20 minutes.

Compare the temperature of the water in the two cans at the end of the 20 minutes. Explain your answer.   [3]

c   Some water is spilt on the bench when the cans are filled. At the end of the experiment the bench is dry.

State what happened to the water on the bench and explain the process in terms of the water molecules.   [3]

[Total: 7]

Cambridge IGCSE Physics (0625) Paper 32, Q5, November 2016

Example student response	Commentary
6 **a** thermal energy transfer	Although the student's answer is not wrong, it is not specific enough to gain the mark. The student should state which type of thermal energy transfer – (infrared) radiation.
	This answer is awarded 0 out of 1 mark.
b The temperature of the cans is higher than before. Silver is better at reflecting heat.	The student has not responded appropriately to the command word 'compare'. They should write a similarity or difference answer between the temperatures of the cans: the black can reach a higher temperature.
	The second statement, which is part of a correct explanation, gains 1 mark. (To gain the other mark, also say that dull black is better at absorbing radiation than shiny silver.)
	This answer is awarded 1 out of 2 marks.

Example student response	Commentary
c Evaporation – some of the molecules escaped from the liquid and went into the air.	The correct statement 'evaporation' gains 1 mark. The student has not given any details about the process. To gain 2 marks for an explanation, they should say that the molecules with more kinetic energy escape from the surface of the liquid (by overcoming the attractive forces between them). *This answer is awarded 1 out of 3 marks.*

7   Now write an improved answer to the parts of Question 6 where you did not score highly. You will need to carefully work back through each part of the question, ensuring that you include enough detail and clearly explain each point. Use the commentary to guide you as you answer.

Now you have read the commentary to the previous question, here is a question on a similar topic which you should attempt. Use the information from the previous response and commentary to guide you as you answer.

8   Figure 8.1 shows equipment used to demonstrate convection in air.
A burning candle is placed beneath glass tube A.

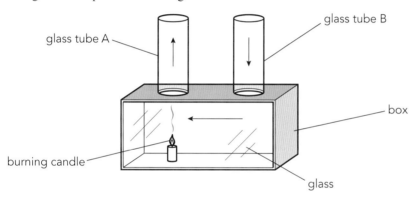

Figure 8.1

a   The arrows in Figure 8.1 show the directions in which air moves.

Explain why the air moves as shown in Figure 8.1.   [3]

b   A student has four rods of identical size. The rods are made of copper, brass, iron and glass.

Describe an experiment to compare thermal conduction along the rods.

You may draw a labelled diagram to help with your answer.   [3]

[Total: 6]

Cambridge IGCSE Physics (0625) Paper 42, Q6, November 2021

The following question has an example student commentary and answer provided. Work through the question first, then compare your answer to the sample answer and commentary. Where were your answers different to the sample answers?

9 **a** A loudspeaker is producing a sound.

Choose words from the box to complete the sentences about sound.

amplitude	frequency	speed	wavelength

   i To increase the loudness of the sound, increase the
   .... of the sound wave. [1]

   ii To increase the pitch of the sound, increase the
   .... of the sound wave. [1]

b Two students determine the speed of sound in air.

The students stand together, 80 m from a large brick wall as shown in Figure 9.1.

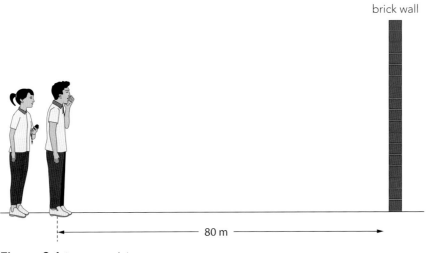

Figure 9.1 (not to scale)

One student shouts and as he shouts the other student starts a stop-watch. She stops the stop-watch when she hears the echo of the shout.

The reading on the stop-watch is 0.56 s.

   i State the **total** distance, in m, the sound travels during the 0.56 s. [1]

   ii Calculate the speed of sound, in m/s, in air using the measurements given in part **b**. [3]

   iii The students' value for the speed of sound is **not** accurate.

   Suggest **two** ways of improving the students' experiment. [2]

[Total: 8]

Adapted from *Cambridge IGCSE Physics (0625) Paper 31, Q8, June 2021*

Example student response	Commentary
9 a i amplitude	This is correct. *This answer is awarded 1 out of 1 mark.*
ii wavelength	This response is incorrect. (Increasing the wavelength would decrease the pitch of the sound.) The correct answer is frequency. *This answer is awarded 0 out of 1 mark.*
b i 80 m	This response is incorrect. The student has failed to realise that the sound wave travels to the wall and back again. *This answer is awarded 0 out of 1 mark.*
ii speed = frequency × wavelength = 0.56 × 80 = 44.8 m/s	The student has written a wave speed formula that is correct but not useful here, because the frequency and wavelength of the sound are not known. (0.56 s is the time, not the frequency; and 80 is not the wavelength but half of the distance travelled.) The formula speed = distance ÷ time needs to be used (and the correct result is 290 m/s). *This answer is awarded 0 out of 3 marks.*
iii Stand further away from the wall and shout louder.	The student's first suggestion is suitable as it is likely to improve the accuracy of the result. The student's second suggestion is unlikely to improve the experiment (since the student with the stop-watch can already hear the shout and its echo). (Other suitable suggestions include: repeat the measurement and average the results; and choose a wall that is far from other walls/buildings.) *This answer is awarded 1 out of 2 marks*

The student failed to answer Questions a ii and b i and b ii correctly in the above example due to misinterpreting the questions. Answer the questions correctly, keeping in mind the guidance given in the commentary.

Now you have read the commentary to the previous question, here is a question on a similar topic which you should attempt. Use the information from the previous response and commentary to guide you as you answer. Note, you should only attempt this question if you are preparing for the Extended exam.

10 a Figure 10.1 shows a transverse wave.

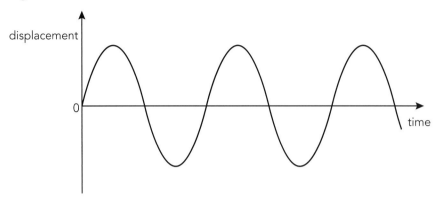

Figure 10.1

On Figure 10.1, draw a wave which has half the amplitude and a greater frequency than the wave shown.   [2]

b A train travels along steel rails. A person waiting at a station hears the sound of the train through the rails before he hears the sound through the air.

    i   Explain why this happens.   [1]

    ii The speed of sound in the rails is 5800 m/s

        Calculate the wavelength of sound of frequency 1100 Hz travelling at this speed.   [2]

[Total: 5]

Cambridge IGCSE Physics (0625) Paper 42, Q6b, c June 2019

13 Light

KNOWLEDGE FOCUS

In this chapter, you will answer questions on:

- reflection of light
- refraction of light
- total internal reflection
- lenses
- dispersion of light.

EXAM SKILLS FOCUS

In this chapter you will:

- practise distinguishing command words from other instructional text.

In most exam questions, the instruction is a command word from the list given in the exam specification. However, other instructions are sometimes used. These include: circle the correct word; underline the correct word; complete the sentence; tick the correct row in a table; draw a diagram; show on a diagram; and label on a diagram.

This type of instruction is simply telling you how to set out your answer on the paper, and the meaning should be obvious. In this chapter you will practise answering questions that use this type of instruction. (If you do not want to write on this book when following instructions such as 'underline' or 'label', you could copy onto separate paper.)

13.1 Reflection of light

1 Figure 13.1 shows a ray diagram created by a student to show how a plane mirror creates an image of an object. The object is represented by an arrow. The student has used the symbol 'i' to mean angle of incidence and 'r' to mean angle of reflection.

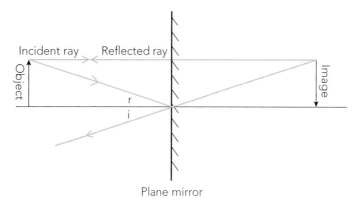

Figure 13.1: Student's diagram of reflection in a plane mirror

a What **three** errors has the student made when drawing this diagram?

b Draw the correct version of the diagram.

2 a State the law of reflection. [1]

b A student holds a large letter B 5 cm in front of a plane mirror. State and explain the apparent distance between the letter and its image. [2]

c Underline all of the terms below that describe the image of the letter B 5 cm in the plane mirror. [2]

virtual   inverted   magnified   laterally inverted   upright   real

[Total: 5]

3 Figure 13.2 shows an object O, represented by a cross, and a plane mirror. Two rays of light from O to the mirror are shown.

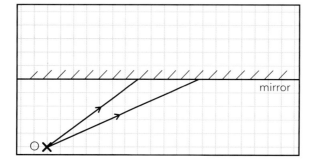

Figure 13.2

a   On the diagram, label the angles incidence 'i'. [1]

b   Complete the ray diagram to show how an image of the object is formed. Show real and virtual rays, and label the image 'I'. [4]

c   A ray of light hits a plane mirror at an angle of 35° to the mirror surface. Determine the angle of reflection. [1]

[Total: 6]

≪ RECALL AND CONNECT 1 ≪

What is the frequency range for normal human hearing?
What is the name for sound that is too high for humans to hear?

UNDERSTAND THESE TERMS

- angle of incidence
- angle of reflection
- incident ray
- laterally inverted
- normal
- real image
- virtual image

13.2 Refraction of light

1   A person looking down at a pond sees a fish. The fish appears to be at position B although it is actually at position A, as shown in Figure 13.3. The figure shows one of the light rays that reaches the person's eye from the fish.

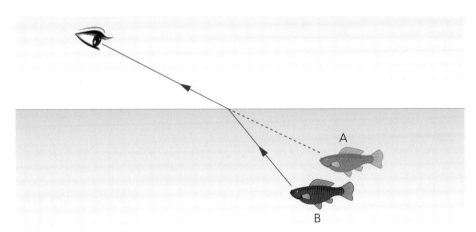

Figure 13.3: A fish under water, and its image as seen by an observer.

a   Why does the light ray bend when it reaches the water surface? Give the name of this phenomenon.

b   Why does the fish appear to be at position A rather than its actual position?

2 A ray of light enters a rectangular block of glass at one side and leaves the block from the opposite side.

a Sketch a ray diagram to show the path of the ray from before it enters the block to after it leaves the block. [3]

A student carries out an experiment to observe a light ray travelling from air into glass. The student varies the angle of incidence and measures the angle of refraction. The student's results table is shown in Table 13.1.

Measurement	Angle of incidence in air, i	Angle of refraction in glass, r	Error in reading?
1	40°	35°	
2	60°	70°	
3	0°	90°	

Table 13.1

b In the table, tick the row(s) in which the student has made an error. Explain how you know. [3]

[Total: 6]

3 A ray of light in air hits a glass block with an angle of incidence of 50°.

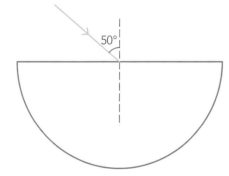

50°

Figure 13.4

a Complete the ray diagram to show the refracted ray of light leaving the glass block. Note: The angle of the refracted ray differs from the angle of incident ray by 20°. [2]

b Calculate the refractive index of the glass. [2]

c Calculate the speed of light in the glass. [2]

[Total: 6]

> **UNDERSTAND THESE TERMS**
> - angle of refraction
> - refraction
> - refractive index
> - speed of light

REFLECTION

Can you now confidently and correctly draw ray diagrams for situations in which light slows down or speeds up when crossing a boundary? If not, how will you work on this?

13.3 Total internal reflection

1   What is total internal reflection, and when does it occur?

2   A doctor uses an endoscope to see inside a patient's stomach in real time.
The endoscope uses optical fibres made of glass.

   a   How do the optical fibres in the endoscope help the doctor to see what is
happening inside the patient's body?

   b   A light ray enters an optical fibre as shown in Figure 13.5. At the end of the
path shown, the incident angle is greater than the critical angle. Copy and
complete the ray diagram to show the path of the ray through the fibre.

Figure 13.5: Ray of light entering an optical fibre

3   Figure 13.6 shows a ray of light entering a diamond.
The diamond is symmetrical.

   a   The refractive index of diamond is 2.4. Calculate the critical angle.   [2]

   A ray of light enters the diamond as shown in Figure 13.6.

   b   Explain why the ray is not refracted at point A.   [1]

   c   Explain why the ray totally internally reflects at point B.   [1]

   d   Draw the path of the ray from point C until it leaves the prism.   [1]

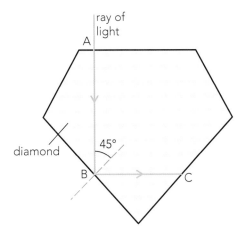

Figure 13.6

   e   Explain, based on the ray diagram you have drawn, why the
diamond looks bright when viewed from above.   [1]

[Total: 6]

« RECALL AND CONNECT 2 «

What is the range of speeds of sound in air? What is an echo?

> **REFLECTION**
>
> The words 'reflection' and 'refraction' are similar. Do you think you will still be able to distinguish between reflection and refraction, and draw correct ray diagrams for them, in the exam? How will you make sure you don't confuse them in future?

13.4 Lenses

1   On squared or graph paper, create a ray diagram showing how a converging lens forms a real image of an object. Draw the object as an arrow, and place it twice as far from the lens as the focal point.

2   Choose the correct words from the box to complete the statements. Each word may be used once, twice or not at all.

> converging   more   less   diverging   thicker   thinner
>
> focal point   focal length   short-sighted   long-sighted

If a person is unable to see distant objects clearly, they are .... This can be corrected by wearing glasses with .... lenses. These lenses are .... in the middle than at the edges.

A different type of lens is used by people who cannot see nearby objects clearly. This type of lens is called a .... lens. It is .... in the middle than at the edges.

In both types of lens, the .... is the distance between the lens and the principal focus or .... A lens with a shorter focal length bends light ...., and so it can be described as .... powerful than a lens with a longer focal length.

3   Sketch the paths of the rays after they pass through the lens in Figure 13.7.   **[Total: 3]**

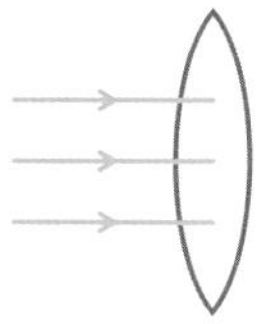

Figure 13.7

4   A magnifying lens is used to make small objects look larger than they really are.

   a   On squared or graph paper, draw a ray diagram to show how a converging lens makes a magnified virtual image of an object. Draw the object as an arrow.   [4]

   b   Compare the heights of the object and the image.   [1]

                                       [Total: 5]

5   Figure 13.8 shows how a lens can be used to correct an eyesight problem.

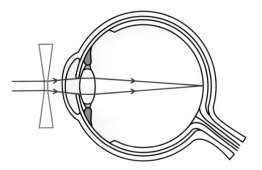

UNDERSTAND THESE TERMS

- converging lens
- diverging lens
- focal length
- focal point
- principal axis

Figure 13.8

a   Identify the eyesight problem.   [1]

b   Name the type of correcting lens used.   [1]

c   Describe where the image is formed if the correcting lens
    is not used.   [1]

[Total: 3]

13.5 Dispersion of light

UNDERSTAND THESE TERMS

- dispersion
- monochromatic
- spectrum

1   Create a diagram to show the dispersion of light by a triangular prism
    made of glass.

2   Identify the colour that is refracted least when white light passes from
    air into glass, and explain why this colour is refracted least.   **[Total: 2]**

SELF-ASSESSMENT CHECKLIST

Let's revisit the Knowledge focus and Exam skills focus for this chapter.

Decide how confident you are with each statement.

Now I can	Show it	Needs more work	Almost there	Confident to move on
use the law of reflection of light to explain how an image is formed in a plane mirror	Describe how an image is formed in a plane mirror. Measure the angle of incidence and reflection to verify the law of reflection.			
construct ray diagrams for reflection	Draw ray diagrams to show the formation of a virtual image in a plane mirror.			
investigate the refraction of light	Describe an experiment to investigate how light is refracted when it passes through a glass block. Draw a diagram to show an example observation.			

CONTINUED

Now I can	Show it	Needs more work	Almost there	Confident to move on
draw ray diagrams to show how lenses form images	Draw labelled ray diagrams to show the formation of real and virtual images by a converging lens.			
describe the difference between real and virtual images	Draw a ray diagram to show formation of real image and a virtual image and state the characteristics of the image.			
describe total internal reflection and how it is used	Complete ray diagrams to show total internal reflection in a glass block and optical fibres.			
describe how the visible spectrum is formed	Draw a diagram to show how white light is dispersed into a spectrum using a glass prism. List the colours of the visible spectrum starting with the colour which is refracted the least.			
practise distinguishing command words from other instructional text.	Write short physics questions using each of the following instructions: label; draw; underline; complete. Write a mark scheme for your questions.			

14 Properties of waves

In this chapter you will practise answering questions that use the command word 'sketch'. It is important that you understand what this command word is instructing you to do:

Sketch	make a simple freehand drawing showing the key features, taking care over proportions.

When you answer the sketch questions in this chapter, remember that you are being asked to do simple freehand drawings and you should not spend too much time trying to make them perfect.

14.1 Describing waves

1   The diagram shows a ripple tank used to observe wave behaviours.

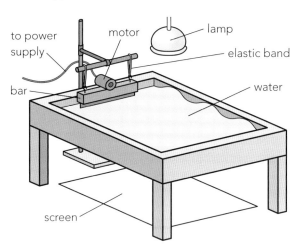

Figure 14.1: Ripple tank

   a   How are straight ripples made in the ripple tank?
       Use the diagram to help you answer.

   b   While straight ripples are travelling across the tank, what is seen on the screen?

   c   How can circular ripples be made in a ripple tank?

2   Around a million earthquakes are measured on Earth every year.
Most of these are not severe enough to be felt by humans.

Fill in the gaps in the sentences using the letters and terms below.

S   P   seismograph   longitudinal
transverse   seismic

To accurately study .... waves, geologists can use a .... that can measure even the slightest ground vibrations that humans cannot feel.

After an earthquake, ... -waves, which are ...., appear on a seismogram first. ....-waves, which are ...., appear later.

3   A student observes a wave on a piece of rope. Figure 14.2 shows two graphs that represent this wave in different ways.

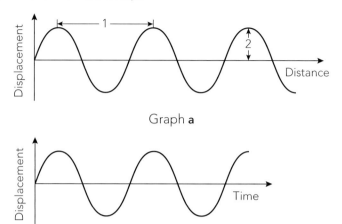

Graph **a**

Graph **b**

Figure 14.2

a   State the quantities represented by each of the arrows, labelled 1 and 2, on Graph **a**.   [2]

b   Explain why Graph **a** is not a suitable type of graph for finding the frequency of the wave.   [1]

c   Describe the method for finding the wave frequency from the type of graph represented in Graph **b**.   [2]

[Total: 5]

4   Compare transverse and longitudinal waves.   **[Total: 2]**

> UNDERSTAND
> THESE TERMS
>
> • longitudinal wave
>
> • transverse wave
>
> • wavelength

≪ RECALL AND CONNECT 1 ≪

What is the difference between the command terms explain and describe?

14.2 Speed, frequency and wavelength

1   Write two equations, each in words and in symbols, for calculating the speed of a wave. Why do they give the same result?

2   Select the correct words to fill the gaps.

When sound waves travel from air to water, the speed .... (increases/ decreases/stays the same). The frequency .... (increases/decreases/stays the same). The wavelength .... (increases/decreases/stays the same).

3 Figure 14.3 shows a position–time graph for a water particle on the surface of the sea.

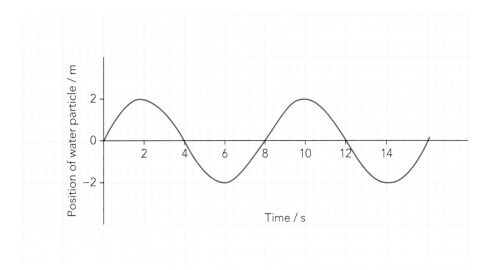

Figure 14.3

a   Determine the frequency of the wave. [2]

b   The wavelength of the wave is 40 m. Calculate the speed of the wave. Write an appropriate unit with your answer. [3]

c   Calculate the time taken for the wave to travel a distance of 1 km. [2]

d   On a copy of the graph, sketch another wave with the same frequency but half the amplitude. [2]

[Total: 9]

REFLECTION

In Question 2, did you remember to check whether your numerical answers were consistent with your knowledge and experience of water waves? Check the answers would you have got if you had incorrectly calculated the speed of the wave using $\dfrac{f}{\lambda}$ or $\dfrac{\lambda}{f}$. Can you tell that each of these answers seems unrealistic?

« RECALL AND CONNECT 2 «

Describe an experiment that uses an electronic timer and two microphones to measure the speed of sound.

14.3 Explaining wave phenomena

1   In a ripple tank, ripples cross a boundary from shallower water to deeper water, and this makes the ripples change direction. Draw a diagram showing the wavefronts before and after the boundary. Draw rays to show the direction of wave travel before and after the boundary.

2   a   An audience member at a concert is sitting behind a pillar. Why can they hear the concert, even though they cannot see it?

   b   An observer is watching the movement of waves around the boats in a harbour. She notices that the waves bend more around small boats than around large boats. Why does this happen?

3   A glass block is placed in a ripple tank. The water above the block all has the same depth, which is less than the depth of the surrounding water. Figure 14.4 shows ripples moving from left to right towards the block.

Figure 14.4

   a   On a copy of the diagram, sketch the wavefronts over and to the right of the glass block.   [2]

   b   The glass block affects the water wave in the same way that a type of lens affects light waves. Name the type of lens.   [1]

   [Total: 3]

≪ RECALL AND CONNECT 3 ≪

What happens when a ray of light travels from air to glass?

SELF-ASSESSMENT CHECKLIST

Let's revisit the Knowledge focus and Exam skills focus for this chapter.

Decide how confident you are with each statement.

Now I can	Show it	Needs more work	Almost there	Confident to move on
describe a wave in terms of speed, amplitude, frequency and wavelength	Label the amplitude, wavelength, crest and trough in a wave and describe the features.			
identify differences between transverse and longitudinal waves.	Explain difference between longitudinal and transverse waves through labelled diagrams.			
calculate wave speed	Calculate wave speeds from data provided			
describe reflection and refraction of waves	Draw diagrams to describe reflection and refraction of waves in a ripple tank when they move from deep to shallow water.			
describe diffraction of waves	Draw diagrams to describe diffraction of waves when they hit a barrier whose gaps have a width that is smaller, equal to or greater than the wavelength of the waves.			
show that I understand the command word 'sketch' and can answer 'sketch' questions.	Write two 'sketch' questions on topics you have previously studied, and show how to answer them.			

15 The electromagnetic spectrum

In this chapter you will practise answering questions that use the command words 'give' and 'identify'. Remember what these command words are instructing you to do.

Give	produce an answer from a given source or recall/memory.
Identify	name/select/recognise.

'Give' questions ask you to either pick out a relevant piece from the information given in the question, or recall a fact that you are expected to know. 'Identify' questions often, though not always, ask you to select one or more answers from a list. These two command words are quite similar. Do not worry about the exact difference between them; with practice you will be able to respond to both of them correctly and confidently.

15.1 Electromagnetic waves

1   A person spends some time outside on a sunny day. They feel warm when the sun shines on them. Later they realise they have sunburn.

   a   What type of radiation makes the person feel warm?

   b   What type of radiation causes sunburn?

   c   Choose the correct word to fill each gap.

   The electromagnetic spectrum is made up of (transverse/longitudinal) waves. These waves all have the same (speeds/frequencies/wavelengths) in a vacuum, but different (speeds/frequencies).

2   Some theme parks now use radio frequency identification (RFID) technology, so that visitors do not need to scan or swipe their tickets. This reduces waiting times.

   a   How does RFID technology work?

   b   If a radio wave has a wavelength of 22 m, what is its frequency in megahertz? (The speed of a radio wave is 3.0×10^8 m/s.)

   c   List two other uses of RFID technology.

3   a   Identify the type of electromagnetic radiation that has the highest frequency, and state one use of this type of radiation in medicine.   [2]

   b   Identify the type of electromagnetic radiation that has wavelengths between those of visible light and microwave radiation. Give one use of this type of radiation in medicine.   [2]

   c   Identify the colour of visible light that has the greatest wavelength.   [1]

   d   Compare the speeds of radio waves and X-rays.   [1]

   [Total: 6]

4   For each of the applications below, give a suitable type of electromagnetic radiation and give one reason why that type of radiation is suitable:

   a   sterilising food   [2]

   b   security cameras for detecting intruders at night   [2]

   c   security marking of valuable equipment.   [2]

   [Total: 6]

UNDERSTAND THESE TERMS
• electromagnetic spectrum
• ultraviolet radiation

≪ RECALL AND CONNECT 1 ≪

What is the difference between red light and violet light?
How can a prism of transparent material disperse light?

15.2 Electromagnetic hazards

1   The Sun emits every type of electromagnetic radiation, but the Earth's atmosphere stops some of this radiation from reaching the ground. Based on this information, why might an astronaut who spends several months inside a space station have an increased likelihood of developing cell mutations?

2   The table lists two uses of electromagnetic radiation. On a copy of the table, identify the type of radiation being used in each activity. For each type of radiation, give one possible harmful effect and describe one suitable safety precaution.

Use	Type of radiation	Possible harmful effect	Safety precaution
sterilising water			
making an image of a broken bone in a person's body			

[Total: 6]

15.3 Communicating using electromagnetic waves

1   a   Which type of electromagnetic radiation is usually used for communicating between Earth and satellites?

    b   Give one advantage and one disadvantage of low orbit satellites compared with geostationary satellites.

2   A satellite is 35 000 km above the Earth's surface.

    a   A person uses a satellite phone to make a call. Calculate the time taken for the signal from their phone to reach a geostationary satellite. (Assume that the satellite is directly above the person. The speed of light is 3.0×10^8 m/s.)   [3]

    b   Explain why the delay in hearing the other person speak will be at least twice as long as the time calculated in part **a**.   [1]

    c   The satellite stays above the same point on the Earth's surface. Give the name of this type of satellite.   [1]

[Total: 5]

3 A person uses a computer to make a phone call.

a The following are used in the process of getting the sound from the person speaking to the person listening:

> optical fibre   amplifier   decoder   encoder
>
> photodiode (for converting light energy to electrical energy)
> regenerator   loudspeaker
>
> laser diode (for converting electrical energy to light energy)
> microphone

Write these in the correct order. [3]

b Identify the device that is used to increase the volume of the sounds heard by the listener. [1]

c Give the function of the encoder. [1]

d State the purpose of the regenerator. [1]

e Give one advantage of transmitting a digital signal instead of an analogue signal over a long distance. [1]

[Total: 7]

> **UNDERSTAND THESE TERMS**
> - analogue signal
> - digital signal

≪ RECALL AND CONNECT 2 ≪

Why are optical fibres used in medicine and telecommunications?

REFLECTION

You have studied the electromagnetic spectrum in detail, including its uses and hazards. Did you notice any overlapping information between previous chapters and this chapter? What connections can you think of between this chapter and chapters 13 and 14? Can you use the connections to help you make sense of, and remember, what you have learned?

SELF-ASSESSMENT CHECKLIST

Let's revisit the Knowledge focus and Exam skills focus for this chapter.

Decide how confident you are with each statement.

Now I can	Show it	Needs more work	Almost there	Confident to move on
describe the main features of the electromagnetic spectrum	List the waves in order of increasing frequency or wavelength. Calculate the frequency of any light in the spectrum using the equation: $v = f\lambda$.			
describe some uses of different electromagnetic waves	Explain why radio waves and microwaves are used in telecommunications, but ultraviolet (UV) rays, x-rays, and gamma rays are used in medicine.			
consider how electromagnetic waves can be used safely	List the safety issues that may arise when using gadgets that produce electromagnetic radiation and list the ways in which harm can be prevented.			
show that I understand the command words 'give' and 'identify' and can answer 'give' and 'identify' questions.	Write two 'give' and two 'identify' exam-style questions on any topic you have revised so far. Ask a classmate to try your questions, and check their answers.			

16 Magnetism

The command words 'predict' and 'comment' are often used in questions about experiments. Remember what these command words are instructing you to do.

Predict	suggest what may happen based on available information.
Comment	give an informed opinion.

Some 'comment' questions ask you to say something about a piece of apparatus used in an experiment. You should respond by saying why it is suitable, or why it is not. Some 'comment' questions ask you to use your physics understanding to respond to an observation, or to a statement made by a student.

One of the three IGCSE Physics assessments focuses on practical skills or knowledge. The other two assessments, particularly the theory paper, can also include questions about experiments. You may be asked to suggest or criticise a method, predict what will be observed, analyse and interpret data, or draw conclusions.

It is often easier to understand and remember a procedure if you have done it yourself. If you encounter an experiment in the exam specification or coursebook that you have not carried out, you may find it helpful to watch a video that demonstrates the experiment.

16.1 Permanent magnets

1 A student loses his way in the woods and uses his compass to navigate home. The compass needle is made of hard steel.

   a How can the student use his compass to navigate home?

   b Why is the compass needle made from hard steel rather than soft iron?

2 a The north pole of a bar magnet is brought close to the south pole of another bar magnet. Predict and explain how the magnets will affect each other.   [2]

   b Figure 16.1 shows a soft iron pin held near the south pole of a bar magnet. The pin becomes magnetised. State the name of this phenomenon.   [1]

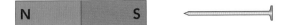

Figure 16.1

   c Predict and explain the direction of the force that acts on the pin because of this phenomenon.   [2]

   d The magnet is taken away, and the pin is brought close to another soft iron pin that has not been near a magnet. Predict and explain what happens.   [2]

[Total: 7]

≪ RECALL AND CONNECT 1 ≪

List the seven types of electromagnetic radiation in order of increasing frequency. For each type, give at least one way in which we use it.

> **UNDERSTAND THESE TERMS**
> - bar magnet
> - permanent magnet

16.2 Magnetic fields

1 A bar magnet has a magnetic field.

   a Where is the magnetic field the strongest?

   b What is the direction of the magnetic field lines?

   c Which of the pieces of apparatus listed below could be used to demonstrate the shape of the magnetic field lines around a bar magnet?

steel pins	iron filings	compass	plain paper
soft iron rod	ammeter	pencil	

   d Draw a diagram to show the magnetic field pattern produced when two bar magnets are placed with south poles facing one another.

2 An electromagnet has a magnetic field as shown in Figure 16.2.

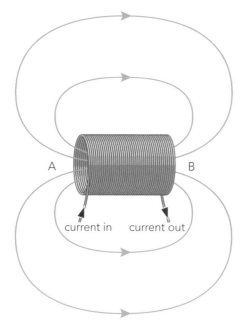

Figure 16.2: A magnetic field around an electromagnet

a What is an electromagnet?

b Which pole is at position A and how can you tell?

3 **a** What three things can be changed to increase the strength of the magnetic field around an electromagnet?

b How can the directions of the field lines of an electromagnet be reversed?

4 A student wants to find out the directions of the magnetic field lines around a bar magnet.

a The student has a plotting compass and some iron filings. She decides to use the plotting compass to investigate the field. Comment on the student's choice. [1]

b Sketch the field lines around a bar magnet, showing the poles of the magnet and direction of the field. [3]

c Another bar magnet is held close to the first bar magnet. The two magnets attract. Sketch the magnetic field in the space between the two magnets. Label the poles. [2]

d A student says that the magnetic field of the Earth is similar to the magnetic field of a bar magnet with the north pole at Earth's north pole. Give one way that this statement is correct and one way that it is not correct. [2]

[Total: 8]

5 A student carries out an experiment to find the relationship between the strength of an electromagnet and the number of turns in its coil. Figure 16.3 shows the apparatus. The student counts the largest number of paperclips the electromagnet can lift, with different numbers of turns in the coil.

a The student has three different sizes of paperclip to choose from and decides to use the smallest size. Comment on the student's choice. [1]

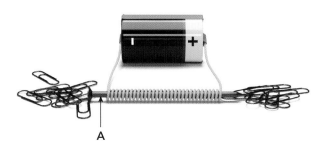

A

Figure 16.3

The table shows the student's results.

Number of coils	Number of paperclips lifted
0	0
10	10
20	18
40	34
60	52

b Plot a suitable graph to show the results. (Use graph paper or squared paper.) [4]

c Describe the relationship between the number of turns and the number of paperclips. [1]

d Predict the number of paperclips the electromagnet can lift if it has 80 turns in its coil. [1]

e Identify the pole at position A in Figure 16.3. [1]

[Total: 8]

REFLECTION

For the graph plotting question, notice how the mark scheme allocates the marks. The requirements will be similar for any graph plotting question in the exam (except that the best fit line will not always be straight). Are there any ways you can improve your graph plotting, to make sure you gain all the available marks next time?

SELF-ASSESSMENT CHECKLIST

Let's revisit the Knowledge focus and Exam skills focus for this chapter.

Decide how confident you are with each statement.

Now I can	Show it	Needs more work	Almost there	Confident to move on
describe magnetic forces between magnets, and between magnets and magnetic materials	Account for induced magnetism. Explain what happens when like poles or unlike poles are brought close and identify magnetic and non-magnetic materials.			
distinguish between hard and soft magnetic materials, and nonmagnetic materials	Describe hard and soft magnetic materials. Give examples of hard and soft magnetic materials with their uses.			
describe an experiment to identify the pattern of magnetic field lines around a bar magnet	Draw the patterns of magnetic field lines around a bar magnet including the direction arrows. Explain how the experiment is conducted using a clear step-by-step method.			
distinguish between the design and use of permanent magnets and electromagnets	Describe the advantage of an electromagnet over a permanent magnet. Suggest situations where each magnet could be utilized.			
show that I understand the command words 'predict' and 'comment' and can answer 'predict' and 'comment' questions.	Choose any physics experiment you have done, and write an exam-style question about that experiment. Include the command words 'predict' and 'comment'. Swap questions with a classmate and write answers.			

17 Static electricity

Remember what this command word is instructing you to do.

Explain	set out purposes or reasons/make the relationships between things evident/provide why and/or how and support with relevant evidence.

Many IGCSE Physics questions use the command word 'explain'. If you are unsure how much detail or depth an 'explain' question is asking for, it is often helpful to look at the number of marks available.

One-mark 'explain' questions can usually be answered with a single statement. There is usually only one possible correct answer, although there might be various ways of expressing it. If an 'explain' question is worth more than one mark, this may be for one or both reasons:

- there is more than one important detail in the answer
- there is more than one essential step in the explanation.

You should not need to write a long paragraph to gain full marks for a single question – but your answer needs to be clear, use scientific terms when appropriate, and not contradict itself.

17.1 Charging and discharging

1 A plastic rod is rubbed with a piece of cloth, giving the rod a negative charge.

    a What kind of charge does the cloth now have?

    b What would happen if another negatively charged rod were brought close to the first rod, and why?

2 A student experiments with static electricity. She knows that when a balloon is rubbed with a piece of wool, the wool becomes positively charged.

    The student rubs a balloon with a piece of wool.

    a State the type of charge on the balloon. [1]

    b Tick one box to complete the sentence below.

        The balloon and the piece of wool now:

        A attract each other.

        B repel each other.

        C do not exert an electrostatic force on each other.

        Explain your choice. [2]

    c Three objects, A, B and C, are each charged. Object A repels object B, and object B repels object C. Compare the types of charge on objects A and C. Justify your answer. [2]

                                        [Total: 5]

> **UNDERSTAND THESE TERMS**
>
> - electrostatic charge
> - negative charge
> - positive charge
> - static electricity

≪ RECALL AND CONNECT 1 ≪

You have learned about magnetic fields and electric fields.
What similarities and differences can you think of?

17.2 Explaining static electricity

1 **a** Give one example of a classroom experiment to demonstrate static electricity.

    b Give one example of a real-life situation in which static electricity is observed.

2 A student holds a rod made of acrylic and rubs it with a cloth made of silk. The rod becomes positively charged.

    a   Explain, in terms of movement of particles, how the rod becomes positively charged. [2]

    b   Deduce whether the rod is an insulator or a conductor. Justify your answer. [3]

    c   The student has another rod which is neutral. He says, 'A neutral object contains no electrons or protons.' Comment on this statement. [2]

[Total: 6]

3 A Van de Graaff generator is a device that builds up a large amount of charge on a metal dome. A girl rests her hand on the dome while it becomes charged, as shown in Figure 17.1.

Figure 17.1

    a   The dome is negatively charged. Explain how an object can have a negative charge. [1]

    b   Suggest why the girl's hairs repel each other. [1]

    c   For the metal dome to become charged, it needs to have a support that is an electrical insulator. Explain why. [2]

    d   The girl takes her hand off the dome and then touches a metal door handle. She receives a small electric shock. Explain why. [1]

[Total: 5]

REFLECTION

In the previous questions, the command word 'explain' appears three times. Compare your answers with the mark scheme. Did you waste time repeating parts of the question ('She receives a small electric shock because…') or writing irrelevant details which were not worth any marks? Did you miss any essential parts of the correct answers? Think about whether you can make any improvements in your approach to explain questions.

UNDERSTAND THESE TERMS

- electrical conductor
- electrical insulator

≪ RECALL AND CONNECT 2 ≪

What similarities and differences are there between good electrical conductors and good thermal conductors?

17.3 Electric fields

1   a   Draw the electric field around a negatively charged sphere.

    b   How would the diagram in a be different if the sphere were positively charged?

2   a   Draw the electric field between two vertical metal plates if the left-hand plate is positively charged and the right-hand plate is negatively charged.   [2]

    b   Give the meaning of the arrows on electric field lines.   [1]

    c   An atom between the two plates does not experience an electrostatic force. Explain why.   [1]

    [Total: 4]

3   a   Give the name of the unit for measuring charge.   [1]

    b   Compare the charges on an electron and a proton.   [2]

    c   A student says that positively charged particles and negatively charged particles will stick to opposite ends of a magnet. Comment on this statement.   [2]

    [Total: 5]

UNDERSTAND THESE TERMS

- coulomb
- electron charge
- proton
- proton charge

SELF-ASSESSMENT CHECKLIST

Let's revisit the Knowledge focus and Exam skills focus for this chapter.

Decide how confident you are with each statement.

Now I can	Show it	Needs more work	Almost there	Confident to move on
investigate the forces between positive and negative charges	Describe how objects with identical or opposite charges affect each other.			
explain static electricity in terms of gaining or losing electrons	Design a variety of experiments to show how objects become charged through friction.			
distinguish between electrical conductors and insulators	Give examples of electrical conductors and electrical insulators and describe how to identify them.			
describe electric fields	Draw electric fields around a charged object.			
show that I understand the command word 'explain', and consider how much detail to give when answering 'explain' questions.	Write three 'explain' questions on topics you have revised so far. Think carefully about how many marks they should be worth and write mark schemes showing how each mark is awarded. Share your ideas with a classmate.			

Exam practice 4

This section contains past paper questions from previous Cambridge exams, which draws together your knowledge on a range of topics that you have covered up to this point. These questions give you the opportunity to test your knowledge and understanding. Additional past paper practice questions can be found in the accompanying digital material.

The following answer has an example student response and commentary provided. Once you have worked through the question, read the student response and commentary. Are your answers different to the sample answers?

1   a   In Figure 1.1, a converging lens projects a sharp image of an object O on to a screen.

Complete the paths of the two rays from the object to the screen.

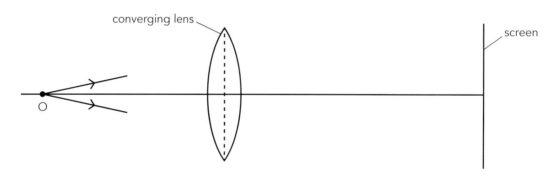

Figure 1.1

[2]

   b   The converging lens in **a** is replaced with a thinner converging lens. The object O and the screen remain in the same positions as in **a**. The thinner converging lens has a longer focal length than the converging lens in **a**.

Complete the paths of the two rays from the object to the screen in Figure 1.2.

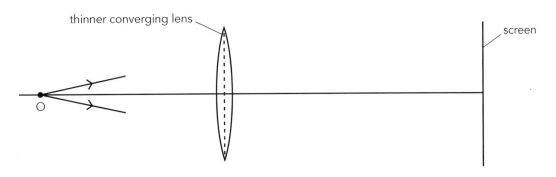

Figure 1.2

[2]

c   A converging lens is used as a magnifying glass.

The focal length of the lens is 10 cm.

   i   Describe the position of the object in relation to the lens.   [1]
   ii   Describe the position of the image in relation to the lens
         and the object.   [1]
   iii Give three properties of the image formed by a magnifying glass.   [2]

[Total: 8]

Cambridge IGCSE Physics (0625) Paper 42, Q7, June 2019

Example student response	Commentary
1 a ![diagram: converging lens, rays from O meeting on Screen] Screen	The student has correctly drawn the rays as straight lines which are bend towards each other by the lens, and meet at the centre line on the screen. In this type of diagram the rays are shown bending at the central line of the lens, not at the edge, but a mark is not deducted for this. *This answer is awarded 2 out of 2 marks.*
b ![diagram: thinner converging lens, rays from O meeting before Screen] Screen	The student has drawn the rays in the same way as in part **a**. This is not correct – a thinner lens bends the rays less strongly. This time the rays will not meet on the screen. *This answer is awarded 0 out of 2 marks.*

Example student response	Commentary
c i between 0 and 10 cm.	The student has correctly used the fact that for a lens to be used as a magnifying glass, the object must be less than one focal length from the lens. *This answer is awarded 1 out of 1 mark.*
ii The image on the same side as the lens. The image is further away from the lens than the object is.	The student's response is correct (and would have gained the mark for either of their two statements). *This answer is awarded 1 out of 1 mark.*
iii Image is virtual and magnified.	This response gives two out of the three correct properties. The mark scheme allows 1 mark for this. *This answer is awarded 1 out of 2 marks.*

2 Now that you've gone through the commentary, try to write an improved answer to the parts of the questions where you lost marks. This will help you check if you've understood why each mark has (or has not) been allocated. Use the commentary to guide you as you answer.

The following answer has an example student response and commentary provided. Once you have worked through the question, read the student response and commentary. Are you answers different to the sample answers?

3 a Figure 3.1 shows crests of a water wave moving from left to right in a harbour.

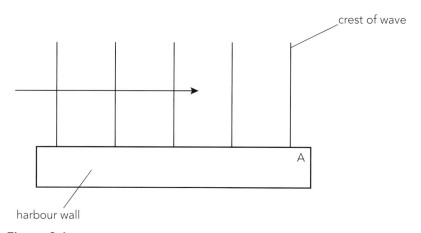

Figure 3.1

    i   On Figure 3.1, draw three more crests to the right of point A.   [2]

    ii State the name of the wave process that occurs as the wave passes point A.   [1]

b Figure 3.2 shows the crests of another wave moving from left to right in a different part of the harbour. This wave moves from deep water to shallow water.

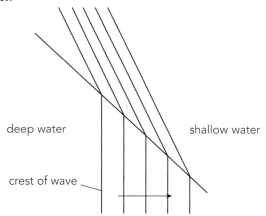

deep water

shallow water

crest of wave

Figure 3.2

i On Figure 3.2, draw an arrow to show the direction of movement of the wave after it has passed into the shallow water. [1]

ii State the name of the process that occurs as the wave passes into the shallow water. [1]

iii Complete Table 3.1 to state whether each of the properties of the wave **increases**, **decreases** or **stays the same** as the wave passes into the shallow water.

Property	Effect
wavelength	
frequency	
speed	

Table 3.1 [3]

[Total: 8]

Cambridge IGCSE Physics (0625) Paper 42, Q6, March 2020

Example student response	Commentary
3 a i 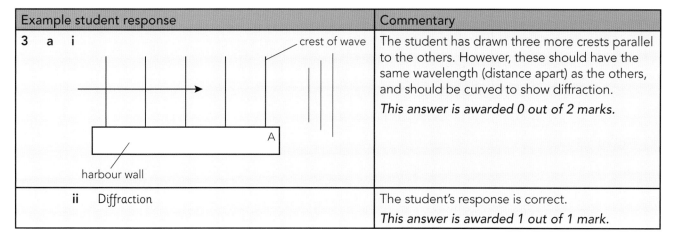 crest of wave	The student has drawn three more crests parallel to the others. However, these should have the same wavelength (distance apart) as the others, and should be curved to show diffraction. *This answer is awarded 0 out of 2 marks.*
ii Diffraction	The student's response is correct. *This answer is awarded 1 out of 1 mark.*

Example student response	Commentary
b i 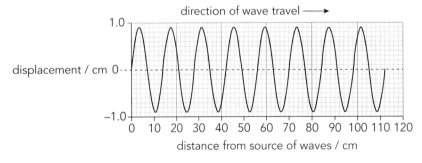 deep water shallow water crest of wave	The arrow is perpendicular to the wave fronts and pointing in the correct direction. *This answer is awarded 1 out of 1 mark.*
ii Refraction	The student's response is correct. *This answer is awarded 1 out of 1 mark.*
iii <table><tr><th>Property</th><th>Effect</th></tr><tr><td>Wavelength</td><td>Increases</td></tr><tr><td>Frequency</td><td>Decreases</td></tr><tr><td>Speed</td><td>Remains the same</td></tr></table>	All three of the student's responses are incorrect. The effect on wavelength can be seen from the diagram, and the effect on speed can also be deduced from this. The frequency of a wave does not change when it changes speed. *This answer is awarded 0 out of 3 marks.*

4   Now write an improved answer to the parts of Question 3 where you did not score highly. You will need to carefully work back through each part of the question, ensuring that you include enough detail and clearly explain each point. Use the commentary to guide you as you answer.

The following answer has an example student response and commentary provided. Once you have worked through the question, read the student response and commentary.

5   Figure 5.1 represents a travelling wave at an instant in time.

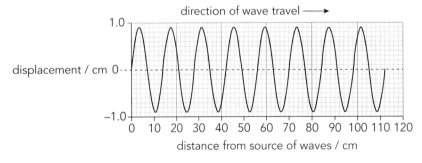

Figure 5.1

a   i   Determine, in cm, the amplitude of the wave.   [1]

    ii   Determine, in cm, the wavelength of the wave.   [2]

    iii It takes 2.0 s for a source to emit the wave shown in Figure 5.1.

         Calculate, in Hz, the frequency of the wave.   [2]

b   Figure 5.2 shows the main regions of the electromagnetic spectrum.

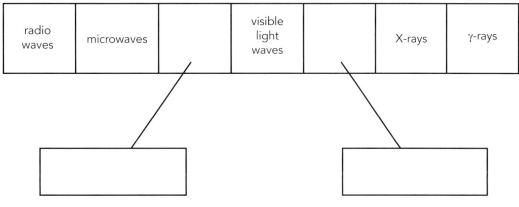

Figure 5.2

    i   Two of the regions are not labelled.

         Add the correct label to each of the unlabelled regions by writing
         in each box.   [2]

    ii   Describe one use of γ-rays.   [1]

Adapted from *Cambridge IGCSE Physics (0625) Paper 32, Q8, March 2020*

Example student response	Commentary
5 a i 1.8 cm	The student has incorrectly taken the amplitude of the wave to be the vertical distance between the peaks and the troughs. *This answer is awarded 0 out of 1 mark.*
ii 112 ÷ 8 = 14 cm	The student's response is correct. (The student has read the distance from the beginning to the end of the wave on the graph, and divided by the number of wavelengths. 2 marks would still be awarded for the correct answer, 14 cm, without a written calculation.) *This answer is awarded 2 out of 2 marks.*
iii 14	The student has simply counted the number of wavelengths in the diagram. This would equal the frequency in Hz if the wave shown were emitted in 1.0 s. However, the question states that it was emitted in 2.0 s. The student needs to calculate the number of wavelengths emitted in one second. *This answer is awarded 0 out of 2 marks.*

Example student response	Commentary
b i red [written in left-hand box] blue [written in right-hand box]	Red and blue light are both part of the visible light region. The unlabelled region on the left represents electromagnetic radiation with a wavelength that is longer than visible light and shorter than microwaves. The unlabelled region on the right represents electromagnetic radiation with a wavelength that is shorter than visible light and longer than X-rays. *This answer is awarded 0 out of 2 marks.*
ii killing bacteria on medical instruments	The student's response is correct (although it does not use the technical term 'sterilising'). *This answer is awarded 1 out of 1 mark.*

6 Now that you've gone through the commentary, try to write an improved answer to the parts of Question 5 where you lost marks. This will help you check if you've understood why each mark has (or has not) been allocated. Use the commentary to guide you as you answer.

The following answer has an example student response and commentary provided. Once you have worked through the question, read the student response and commentary.

7 This question is about the magnetic fields around bar magnets. Figure 7.1 shows two positions used by a student doing an experiment.

Figure 7.1

a Figure 7.2 shows a magnet, labelled magnet 1, placed on position 1.

Figure 7.2

On Figure 7.2, draw lines to show the pattern of the magnetic field produced by magnet 1. Place arrows on the lines to show the direction of the field. [3]

b   Magnet 1 is removed from position 1. Figure 7.3 shows another magnet, labelled magnet 2, placed on position 2.

Figure 7.3

On Figure 7.3, draw, at the right-hand end of position 1, a line with an arrow to show the direction of the magnetic field produced by magnet 2.   [1]

c   Figure 7.4 shows magnet 1 placed on position 1 and magnet 2 placed on position 2.

Figure 7.4

i   State the direction of the force that the N pole of magnet 2 exerts on the N pole of magnet 1.   [1]

ii   Justify your answer to **c i**.   [1]

[Total: 6]

Cambridge IGCSE Physics (0625) Paper 42, Q7, November 2022

Example student response	Commentary
7 a (diagram showing a magnet with S on left, N on right, and a single field line arc with arrow pointing left above the magnet)	The student has drawn one correct line with the correct arrow direction. However, this is a very incomplete field diagram. To get the marks, they needed to draw at least two field lines meeting each pole, including at least one complete loop above and below the magnet, and at least two correct arrows. *This answer is awarded 0 out of 3 marks.*
b (diagram showing position 1 rectangle, an arrow pointing left, and a magnet labelled N on left, S on right)	The student's response correctly shows that the magnetic field points away from the north pole, towards the left. *This answer is awarded 1 out of 1 mark.*
i towards the left	The student's response is correct. *This answer is awarded 1 out of 1 mark.*
ii because north poles repel	Although the student's statement is true, it does not gain the mark. The underlying reason why the force on magnet 1 is to the left is that the force on a north pole in a magnetic field is in the direction of the field lines. *This answer is awarded 0 out of 1 mark.*

8 Now write an improved answer to the parts of Question 7 where you did not score highly. You will need to carefully work back through each part of the question, ensuring that you include enough detail and clearly explain each point. Use the commentary to guide you as you answer.

The following question has an example student commentary and answer provided. Work through the question first, then compare your answer to the sample answer and commentary. Where were your answers different to the sample answers?

9 a i State what is meant by the *direction* of an electric field. [1]

   ii Figure 9.1 shows a pair of oppositely charged horizontal metal plates with the top plate positive.

Figure 9.1

The electric field between the plates in Figure 9.1 is uniform.
Draw lines on Figure 9.1 to represent this uniform field.
Add arrows to these lines to show the direction of the field. [3]

b Figure 9.2 shows a very small negatively charged oil drop in the air between a pair of oppositely charged horizontal metal plates.
The oil drop does not move up or down.

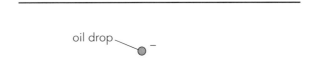

Figure 9.2

   i Suggest, in terms of forces, why the oil drop does not move up or down. [2]

   ii Without losing any of its charge, the oil drop begins to evaporate.
State and explain what happens to the oil drop. [2]

[Total: 8]

Cambridge IGCSE Physics (0625) Paper 42, Q9, March 2016

Example student response	Commentary
9 a i The direction of an electric field is the way the arrows on the field lines point.	The student's response states how the direction of an electric field is shown in a diagram but does not give its meaning. The direction of an electric field is the direction of the force on a positive charge. *This answer is awarded 0 out of 1 mark.*
ii + + + + + + + + + + + + + (field lines diagram pointing downward)	The student's response correctly shows that the field lines are vertical and parallel, and that the arrows point downwards (in the direction of the force on a positive charge). However, the field between two plates is uniform (and the question also states this), which means that the field lines should be equally spaced. *This answer is awarded 2 out of 3 marks.*
b i The forces balance.	This response is correct but not detailed enough to gain both marks. The student has not stated the types or causes of the forces (upward force due to the electric field and downward force due to the drop's weight). *This answer is awarded 1 out of 2 marks.*
ii The drop gets smaller because it is gradually turning from liquid to gas.	The student has misunderstood the question. The question already states that the drop evaporates, and the student's answer describes evaporation instead of stating and explains what now happens to the drop. The weight of the drop decreases (because its mass decreases), so the upward force is greater than the downward force. Therefore the drop accelerates upwards. *This answer is awarded 0 out of 2 marks.*

Now you have read the commentary to the previous question, here is a question on a similar topic which you should attempt. Use the information from the previous response and commentary to guide you as you answer.

10 a A student rubs a polythene rod with a dry cloth. The polythene rod becomes negatively charged.

Describe and explain how the rod becomes negatively charged. [3]

b The negatively charged polythene rod hangs from a nylon thread so that it is free to turn.

The student charges a second polythene rod and brings it close to the first rod, as shown in Figure 10.1.

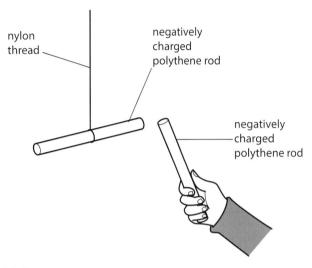

nylon
thread

negatively
charged
polythene rod

negatively
charged
polythene rod

Figure 10.1

Describe and explain what happens when the negatively charged rods are close to each other. [2]

[Total: 5]

Cambridge IGCSE Physics (0625) Paper 32, Q11, March 2018

18 Electrical quantities

Remember what this command word is instructing you to do.

Calculate	work out from given facts, figures or information.

It is important to show your working when doing a calculation question. This usually involves writing:

- the equation you are going to use
- a rearranged version of the equation, if needed
- the actual calculation you will do (showing the values substituted into the equation)
- the calculated quantity with a unit.

Showing your working increases your chances of gaining marks. It also helps you to think clearly, and makes it easier to check your work afterwards.

After you answer a question that involves a calculation, it can be helpful to check whether your result fits any expectations you may have. In areas of physics that are familiar from everyday life or from your studies so far, such as the behaviours of water waves and sound waves, you may be able to recognise when an answer is unrealistic.

For example, if you calculated an ocean wave speed of 1000 m/s you might notice, from your physics knowledge or observations of ocean waves in real life or in videos, that 1 km/s seemed unrealistically fast. You would then check your calculation for errors.

18.1 Current in electric currents

1 A cell, switch and lamp are connected in series, as shown in Figure 18.1.

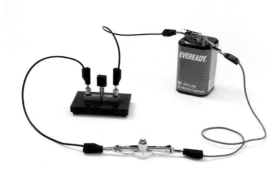

Figure 18.1: Simple electric circuit

a What type of energy store does a cell have?

b What type of useful energy transfer happens in a cell?

c Complete the sentences below using appropriate words from the box.
Each word may be used once, more than once, or not at all.

positive	negative	insulator	open
closed	cell	conductor	battery

In a circuit diagram, two lines, one longer and the other shorter and thicker,
are used to represent a .... The shorter line of the symbol represents
the .... terminal and the longer line represents the ....
terminal. Two or more of these devices connected in series are called
a ....

Current flows when the switch is .... The wires carrying current are
made of metal, which is a good electrical .... The coating around
the wires is made of plastic, which is a good electrical ....

2 Figure 18.2 shows two types of ammeter.

a What are the names of each of these types of ammeter?

b What quantity does an ammeter measure, and what is the SI unit for this
quantity?

c What do the letters 'd.c.' mean on the left-hand ammeter?

d Why does the left-hand ammeter have two black connectors and two
different scales?

Figure 18.2: Two types
of ammeter

3   A cell, ammeter and lamp are connected as shown in Figure 18.3.

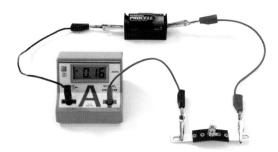

Figure 18.3

a   Draw a circuit diagram for the circuit shown in Figure 18.3.   [2]
    The reading on the ammeter is −0.16 A.

b   Explain why the reading is negative.   [1]

c   State the current in the wire connecting the lamp to the cell.
    Explain your answer.   [2]

[Total: 5]

4   a   Sketch a series circuit containing a cell and a lamp. On the diagram,
        mark the directions of electron flow and conventional current.   [2]

    b   Calculate the charge that flows through a lamp in one minute
        if the current in the lamp is 0.60 A.   [3]

    c   There is a current of 300 mA in a resistor. Calculate the time taken,
        in minutes, for a charge of 90 C to flow through the resistor.   [3]

[Total: 8]

《 RECALL AND CONNECT 1 《

Give two examples of electrical conductors and two examples of electrical
insulators. How do conductors conduct electricity?

**UNDERSTAND
THESE TERMS**

- alternating current
- ammeter
- battery
- cell
- current
- direct current
- galvanometer

18.2 Voltage in electric circuits

1 **a** What is the function of a voltmeter?

b How is a voltmeter connected in a circuit?

c Draw a series circuit with a lamp, a resistor, and a battery made of three 1.5 V cells in series. Add an ammeter and voltmeter to the circuit showing how to measure the current in the battery and the potential difference across the battery.

d What is the e.m.f. of the battery?

e Say what this e.m.f. means in terms of energy transfer.

2 **a** How much energy does 5.0 C of charge gain when it passes through a 1.5 V battery?

b If 14 J of energy is transferred to a lamp when 2 C of charge passes through it, what is the potential difference across the lamp?

3 **a** Compare electromotive force (e.m.f.) and potential difference (p.d.). [2]

b Figure 18.4 shows an electric circuit containing two lamps and a cell. Both lamps are lit.

The e.m.f. of the cell is 2 V. Deduce whether the potential difference across lamp 1 is greater than, less than or equal to 2 V. Justify your answer. [2]

[Total: 4]

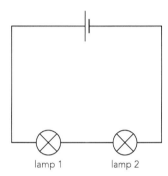

lamp 1   lamp 2

Figure 18.4

4 **a** State the relationship between e.m.f., charge and energy transferred. [1]

b A charge of 5.0 C flows through a battery. The e.m.f. of the battery is 3.0 V. Calculate the energy transferred, and state whether it is transferred to the battery or from the battery. [3]

c A lamp in a circuit has a potential difference of 5.0 V. The current in the lamp is 2.0 A. Calculate the energy transferred to the lamp in 10 s. [4]

[Total: 8]

≪ RECALL AND CONNECT 2 ≪

An insulating rod becomes positively charged by friction.
How does the transfer of particles make the rod positive?

UNDERSTAND THESE TERMS

- electromotive force
- potential difference
- voltage

18.3 Electrical resistance

1   Choose the correct words to complete the statements.

   a   A student has two pieces of wire with the same cross-sectional area. Wire Y is longer than wire X. The resistance of Y is greater than/less than/equal to the resistance of X.

   b   A student has two pieces of wire with the same length. Wire Y has a larger cross-sectional area than wire X. The resistance of Y is greater than/less than/equal to the resistance of X.

2   A circuit is set up as shown in Figure 18.5.

   For different values of the e.m.f. of the power supply, a student measures the potential difference across the resistor and the current in the circuit. The table shows the results.

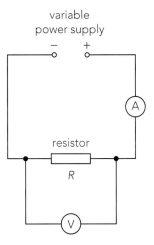

Potential difference / V	Current / A
2.5	0.11
5.0	0.20
10	0.38
15	0.59

   Use the readings to calculate the resistance of the resistor. Include the appropriate unit in your answer.   [Total: 4]

Figure 18.5

3   A circuit is set up as shown in Figure 18.6.

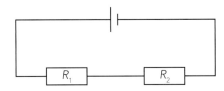

Figure 18.6

   a   The current in resistor R_1 is 0.80 A. State the current in resistor R_2.   [1]

   b   The potential difference across R_2 is 0.50 V. Calculate the resistance of R_2.   [2]

   c   A third resistor is added, in series with R_1 and R_2. Predict and explain how this affects the current in the cell.   [2]

   [Total: 5]

UNDERSTAND THIS TERM

• resistance

18.4 More about electrical resistance

1 a The potential difference across a lamp in a circuit is 1.5 V. The resistance of the lamp is 5.0 Ω. What is the current in the bulb?

   b What potential difference must be applied across a 50 Ω resistor to make a current of 0.10 A flow through it?

2 Sketch the current–voltage characteristic for a diode.

3 A student wants to investigate the relationship between potential difference and current for a filament lamp.

   a Sketch a suitable circuit, including a variable voltage power supply. [2]

   The student obtains the readings shown in the table below.

Potential difference / V	Current / A
1.0	0.10
2.0	0.20
3.0	0.25
4.0	0.28
5.0	0.30

   b Plot a graph of current against voltage. (Use squared paper or graph paper.) [4]

   c Describe the relationship between potential difference and current for the lamp. [2]

   d Explain the relationship between potential difference and current. [3]

   [Total: 11]

4 A student has a 400 cm piece of copper wire with uniform cross-sectional area. Its resistance is 0.32 Ω.

   a The student cuts a 100 cm piece of this wire. Determine its resistance. [1]

   b Another student has some thinner copper wire, with half as much cross-sectional area. Determine the resistance of a 100 cm piece of this wire. [1]

   [Total: 2]

UNDERSTAND THIS TERM

• ohmic resistor

18.5 Electrical energy, work and power

≪ RECALL AND CONNECT 3 ≪

What are the definitions of work and power, and how are these two quantities related?

1   What is the equation for electrical power in words and in symbols, and what is the SI unit of each quantity in the equation?

2   A mobile phone (cell phone) is connected to a power supply of 120 V to be charged. While the phone is charging, a current of 0.10 A flows.

   a   Calculate the power used to charge the phone.   [2]
   b   Calculate the energy transferred to the phone per minute, in:
      i   joules   [2]
      ii   kilowatt-hours.   [2]
   c   Calculate the total cost of charging the mobile phone for 30 minutes every day for 30 days if the cost per unit (kilowatt-hour) is US $0.10.   [3]

[Total: 9]

3   When a freezer is running, the potential difference across it is 220 V and the current flowing through it is 0.75 A. Calculate the energy, in joules, transferred to the freezer in 10 s.   **[Total: 4]**

UNDERSTAND THIS TERM
• electrical power

REFLECTION

Did you notice that there were four marks for Question 3? It required a longer calculation using two equations.

To answer calculation questions successfully, you need to be able to recall the relevant equations, choose the appropriate equation(s) to solve a problem, rearrange equations when necessary, convert quantities between different units (such as mA and A) when necessary, and carry out the calculations accurately. Think about each of these skills – are there any that you particularly need to work on?

SELF-ASSESSMENT CHECKLIST

Let's revisit the Knowledge focus and Exam skills focus for this chapter.

Decide how confident you are with each statement.

Now I can	Show it	Needs more work	Almost there	Confident to move on
learn about electric current, resistance and voltage	Draw a circuit diagram for a circuit that could be used to measure current, resistance and voltage. Define the key terms in your own words. Identify the units for each key term.			
describe an experiment to determine resistance using ammeters and voltmeters	Design an experiment to measure current and potential difference and evaluate resistance from the results.			
learn how the resistance of a wire relates to its length and diameter	Explain how the resistance of a wire relates to its length and area.			
understand that energy is transferred from the power source to the circuit components	Calculate electrical power and energy using values of circuit components. Write equations linking energy, power, current and potential difference.			
calculate resistance, electrical power, energy and the cost of electrical energy	Write a short guide for IGCSE Physics students on how to calculate resistance, electrical power, energy, and the cost of electrical energy.			
show that I understand the command word 'calculate' and understand the importance of showing my working clearly when answering 'calculate' questions.	Check your workings for the 'calculate' questions in this chapter against the answers and note any steps that you missed or any errors you made. Summarise what you can do to improve.			

19 Electrical circuits

In this chapter you will answer questions using the command word 'suggest'. The 'suggest' command word can be used in two different ways: there may be no definitive answer or you may need to draw upon wider knowledge to deal with an unfamiliar context.

Suggest	apply knowledge and understanding to situations where there are a range of valid responses in order to make proposals/put forward considerations.

Many 'suggest' questions cannot be answered by simply recalling something you have learned, because they often involve contexts or ideas you have not encountered or thought about before. You may need to spend a little more time on a 'suggest' question than on a 'state,' 'describe' or 'explain' question, to think about how your physics knowledge and understanding can be applied to this new situation.

19.1 Circuit components

1   A circuit diagram that includes an LDR is shown in Figure 19.1.

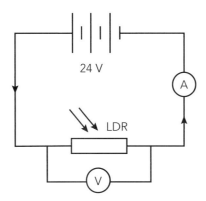

Figure 19.1: LDR circuit

a   What does 'LDR' stand for?

b   What happens to the readings on the ammeter and voltmeter in the circuit if the light level increases, and why?

c   How are LDRs used?

d   An electrical component has a resistance that decreases when the temperature increases. What is the name of this component?

2   a   What is an LED, and how does it behave in a circuit?

b   List two advantages of using LEDs instead of filament lamps in traffic lights.

3   Figure 19.2 shows a relay circuit used to operate a warning lamp on the outside of an industrial refrigerator.

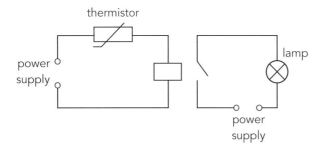

Figure 19.2

The lamp lights if the temperature inside the refrigerator is too high.
Explain how this works.   **[Total: 4]**

≪ RECALL AND CONNECT 1 ≪

What are e.m.f. and p.d.? What is the relationship between resistance, current and potential difference for a component in an electric circuit?

19.2 Combinations of resistors

1   Figure 19.3 shows a circuit containing six lamps.
    Answer the following questions without doing any calculations.

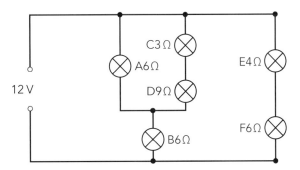

Figure 19.3 Resistors in series and parallel

a   Is the current greater in lamp C or D, or the same in both?
    How do you know?
b   Is the current greater in lamp E or in the power supply, or the same in both?
    How do you know?

2   Calculate the combined resistance of the circuit shown in Figure 19.3.

3 Complete each statement by choosing the correct phrase in brackets.

In a series circuit, the total potential difference across all of the components equals the (difference between/sum of/average of) the individual potential differences across each component.

In a parallel circuit, the sum of the currents into a junction equals the (difference between/sum of/average of) the currents out of the junction.

For two parallel branches in a circuit, the (currents in/potential differences across/ resistances of) the branches are the same.

4 Three resistors and a cell are connected as shown in Figure 19.4. An ammeter and voltmeter are included in the circuit.

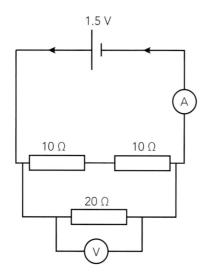

Figure 19.4

   a State the combined resistance of the two 10 Ω resistors.   [1]

   b State whether the current in the cell is greater, less than, or the same as the current in the 20 Ω resistor. Explain your answer.   [2]

   c The branch containing the 20 Ω resistor is removed from the circuit. Predict whether the reading on the ammeter will increase, decrease or stay the same. Explain your answer.   [2]

   [Total: 5]

5 This question is about the circuit shown in Figure 19.4.

   a Calculate the combined resistance of the three resistors.   [3]

   b Predict the reading on the voltmeter.   [1]

   c Calculate the current in the 20 Ω resistor.   [2]

   d Calculate the potential difference across one of the 10 Ω resistors.   [2]

   e Calculate the reading on the ammeter.   [1]

   [Total: 9]

6   A student sets up the circuit shown in Figure 19.5.

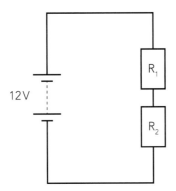

Figure 19.5

a   The potential difference across resistor R_1 is 8 V. Resistor R_2 has resistance 40 Ω. Calculate the resistance of R_1.   [3]

b   The student replaces resistor R_2 with an LDR. She connects a voltmeter in parallel with the LDR and uses the voltmeter reading as a light level indicator.

State and explain whether the voltmeter reading increases or decreases when the light level increases.   [2]

[Total: 5]

> **UNDERSTAND THIS TERM**
>
> • potential divider

《 RECALL AND CONNECT 2 《

What are the quantities in the equation $I = \dfrac{Q}{t}$, what is the standard unit of each quantity, and when would you use this equation arranged in this way? What are the quantities and their units in the equation $V = \dfrac{W}{Q}$ and when is the equation used in this arrangement?

19.3 Electrical safety

1   A 2 kW water heater is powered by a 220 V mains supply in a person's home.

a   The person thinks a 9 A fuse would be suitable for the plug connected to the water heater. Do you agree, and why?

b   Bathroom light switches are often outside the room, or inside the room but operated by a cord hanging from the ceiling. Why is this?

2   What is the purpose of:

a   including a fuse in a circuit

b   including a trip switch in a circuit

c   earthing an electrical appliance

d   double insulating an electrical appliance?

3   Figure 19.6 shows a diagram of a three-pin plug and its connections to an appliance.

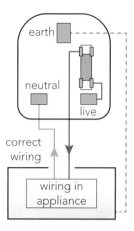

Figure 19.6

a   Give a reason why the fuse could melt. [1]

b   The fuse inside the plug is connected to the live wire. Suggest why the fuse should not be connected to the neutral wire instead. [2]

c   The outer casing of the appliance is connected to the earth pin of the plug. Explain how this protects users of the appliance. [3]

d   In a building, the wire leading from the earth connection in an electric socket is connected to a plastic water pipe that leads into the ground. Suggest why this is not appropriate. [2]

[Total: 8]

UNDERSTAND THESE TERMS
• double insulated
• earthed
• trip switch

≪ RECALL AND CONNECT 3 ≪

Write the equation for electrical power, and the general equation for power. What is the relation between 1 W and 1 J?

REFLECTION

Try timing yourself when answering questions from this chapter. What was your average time? If it was long, was it because you find this topic difficult or because that is your normal working pace?

If you need to improve your pace or your ability to work well under time pressure, you could try any of the following: working through past paper practice sections from this book under timed conditions working through past papers within the time allowed in the real exam; and reminding yourself, whenever you work on exam-style questions, to work with a slight sense of urgency rather than at a completely relaxed pace. What strategies will you use?

SELF-ASSESSMENT CHECKLIST

Let's revisit the Knowledge focus and Exam skills focus for this chapter.

Decide how confident you are with each statement.

Now I can	Show it	Needs more work	Almost there	Confident to move on
draw and interpret circuit diagrams	Test yourself on the electrical symbols you need to know. (You can find these in the exam specification). Draw a diagram of a circuit that has a d.c. supply connected to a lamp and a resistor in parallel.			
describe how current and resistance vary in different circuits	Calculate resistance in a series and parallel circuit. Explain why current is equal in a series circuit, but is divided in a parallel circuit.			
highlight the hazards of using electricity and describe and explain electrical safety measures, including fuses, circuit breakers, and earth wires	Show how fuses, trip switches and double insulation work. Explain the benefits of earthing for any electrical appliance. Select appropriate fuse ratings and circuit breaker settings.			
learn how to calculate resistance, currents and voltages in circuits	Determine the values of effective resistance of a circuit, along with values of voltage and current.			
describe the action of diodes and potential divider circuits	State the use of diodes and LED's and describe how they work.			
show that I understand the command word 'suggest' and can answer 'suggest' questions.	Answer the 'suggest' questions in this chapter and compare your answers with the mark scheme.			

20 Electromagnetic forces

It is quite common for an exam question to use two command words, one of which is often 'explain', such as: 'state and explain', 'describe and explain' or 'predict and explain'. You should take particular care to make sure you respond to both command words. Make sure you cover both command words in your answers to answer the questions well.

20.1 The magnetic effect of a current

≪ RECALL AND CONNECT 1 ≪

Describe a method for investigating the pattern of magnetic field lines around a bar magnet.

1 Current flows through a straight wire as shown in Figure 20.1.
Field lines have been drawn around the wire, but the arrows are missing.

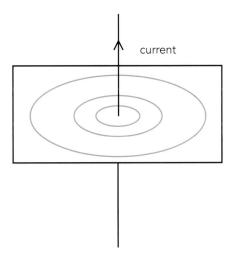

Figure 20.1: Magnetic field around a wire

a What rule can be used to find the direction of the field lines around a wire?

b In which direction should arrows be drawn on the magnetic field lines in Figure 20.1?

The wire is now wound around a cylindrical tube to make a solenoid as shown in Figure 20.2.

c How can you find which end of a solenoid is the north pole?

d At which end of the solenoid in Figure 20.2, A or B, is there a north pole?

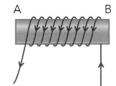

Figure 20.2: Solenoid

2 Complete the statements below, using one word to fill each gap.

In a solenoid, field lines emerge from the .... pole and enter the .... pole. The polarity of the field around a solenoid depends on the .... of current flow at each end of the coil.

The closer the field lines, the .... the magnetic field. Outside the coil, the field lines are closest together near the .... Inside the coil, the field lines are .... to each other. To increase the strength of the field, increase the number of .... in the coil or increase the ....

3   Figure 20.3 shows a relay used to switch a motor on and off.

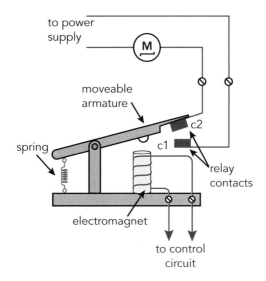

Figure 20.3

a   Suggest a suitable material for the armature. Justify your choice.   [2]

b   A person presses a switch that completes the control circuit.
Describe and explain what happens.   [3]

c   Suggest why a spring is used to attach the armature to the base.   [2]

d   Suggest one reason why an electromagnetic relay is used, instead
of a simple switch, to start the motor.   [1]

[Total: 8]

> **UNDERSTAND THESE TERMS**
> - armature
> - right–hand grip rule

20.2 Force on a current-carrying conductor

1   Figure 20.4 shows a circuit that is completed by a copper rod that rests on two
supports, without being attached to them. The rod lies in the magnetic field
between two magnets.

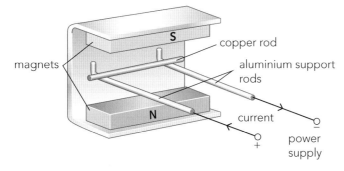

Figure 20.4: Current-carrying rod in a magnetic field

a   What happens to the copper rod when a current flows through it, and why?

b   What could be changed to reverse the direction of the force acting on the copper rod? Give two possible answers.

c   Copper and aluminium are not magnetic materials. Why do you think non-magnetic materials have been chosen for this demonstration?

2   How can Fleming's left-hand rule be used to predict the direction of the force on a current-carrying conductor in a magnetic field?

3   Figure 20.5 shows a cross-section of a loudspeaker.

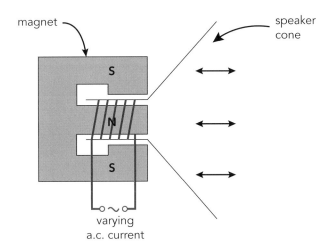

Figure 20.5

a   Write the correct order of the steps below to show how the loudspeaker works.   [2]

   A   This causes a changing magnetic field around the coil.

   B   The movement of the speaker cone creates sound waves.

   C   There is an alternating current in the coil.

   D   The coil vibrates, making the attached speaker cone vibrate.

   E   The coil is alternately attracted to and repelled by the permanent magnet.

b   Predict and explain what will happen if direct current flows in the coil instead of alternating current.   [2]

c   Describe the useful energy stores and transfers involved when the loudspeaker is operating.   [3]

[Total: 7]

《 RECALL AND CONNECT 2 《

What is a Sankey diagram? Make a sketch of a Sankey diagram to show energy transfer in a television.

UNDERSTAND THESE TERMS

- Fleming's left-hand rule
- motor effect

20.3 Electric motors

1   List three ways of increasing the turning effect on a current-carrying coil in a magnetic field.

2   Figure 20.6 shows the magnets and coil of an electric motor. The upwards and downwards arrows show the directions of the forces acting sides AB and CD of the motor's coil.

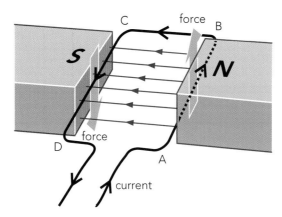

Figure 20.6: Coil and magnets of an electric motor

a   Name the rule that can be used to find the direction of the force on a current-carrying wire in a magnetic field.

b   Why does the coil in Figure 20.6 rotate?

c   Why are there no forces on sides AD and BC of the coil?

d   List three uses of an electric motor.

3   Figure 20.7 shows a simple direct current (d.c.) motor that is connected to a cell. The coil has many turns, but only one of the turns is shown here.

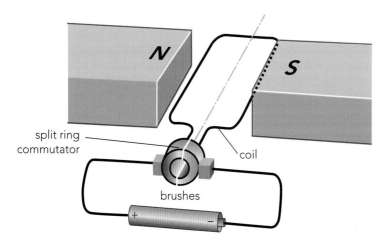

Figure 20.7

a   The brushes are made of graphite, which is a slippery material. Explain why it is useful for the brushes to have low friction. [2]

b   Explain why the commutator is split, instead of being a complete ring. [1]

c   State the direction of the magnetic field in Figure 20.7. [1]

d   State the direction of flow of conventional current in Figure 20.7. [1]

e   State and explain whether the coil rotates clockwise or anticlockwise, as seen when looking towards the coil from the commutator. [2]

f   State the effect, if any, of making each of these changes to the motor in Figure 20.7:

   i   adding more turns to the coil [1]

   ii   using weaker magnets [1]

   iii swapping the brushes so that they are in contact with opposite sides of the commutator. [1]

g   While the motor is running, energy is transferred usefully from the energy store of the cell to the energy store of the motor. Identify these energy stores. [2]

[Total: 12]

> **UNDERSTAND THIS TERM**
> * commutator

REFLECTION

How did you find the Exam skills questions in this chapter that contained more than one command word? Did you make sure you responded to both command words in your answers? How can you ensure that you do this in the exam?

20.4 Beams of charged particles and magnetic fields

1   A beam of electrons is about to enter a magnetic field, as shown in Figure 20.8. The crosses show that the magnetic field direction is into the page.

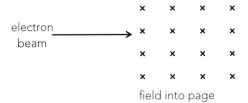

Figure 20.8: Electron beam entering a magnetic field

a   What is the direction of the current?

b   Draw the path of the electric beam as it passes through the magnetic field.

c   The direction of the magnetic field is reversed. What is the effect on the path of the electron beam?

2 A beam of electrons travels into a magnetic field, as shown in Figure 20.9.

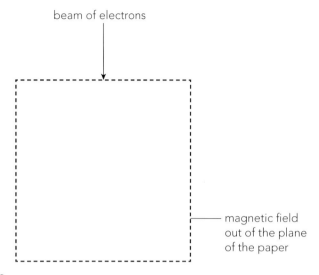

beam of electrons

magnetic field
out of the plane
of the paper

Figure 20.9

a On a copy of the diagram, sketch the path of the electron beam after
it enters the magnetic field. Continue the line to show the path of the
beam after it leaves the magnetic field. [2]

b Describe, and explain in terms of current, the path the beam will take
through the magnetic field if the electrons are replaced by:

i positive particles [2]

ii neutral particles. [2]

[Total: 6]

《 RECALL AND CONNECT 3 《

What does it mean for two electrical components to be connected 'in series'
or 'in parallel' with each other? Summarise the relationships between currents
and potential differences in components connected in series and parallel.

REFLECTION

This chapter involves abstract concepts, including magnetic fields and their field
lines. How will you make sure you understand and can apply these ideas? When
you practise recalling these concepts, do you find it most helpful to write about
them, talk about them, make sketches, or use actions or gestures?

After learning the concepts, how will you assess whether you understand them?
Take a few minutes to think about this and make a plan.

SELF-ASSESSMENT CHECKLIST

Let's revisit the Knowledge focus and Exam skills focus for this chapter.

Decide how confident you are with each statement.

Now I can	Show it	Needs more work	Almost there	Confident to move on
investigate the magnetic fields around current–carrying conductors	Describe an experiment to show the magnetic field around a current-carrying wire. Sketch the magnetic field around a current-carrying wire.			
observe the force on a current-carrying conductor in a magnetic field	Describe or carry out an experiment to observe the force on a current-carrying conductor in a magnetic field.			
describe the principle of an electric motor and lit ways of increasing its strength	Explain to a friend or family member the concept of an electric motor, and describe some uses of motors. List ways to increase the turning effect on the coil.			
describe the factors affecting the strength and direction of electromagnetic fields and forces	Describe how to change the field strength and direction of the magnetic field around a solenoid. Create an exam-style question asking for the direction of the force on a current-carrying wire in a magnetic field.			
show that I can answer questions that include two command words.	Check your answers to the Exam skills questions in this chapter that use two command words. Identify which part of the answer is responding to which command word.			

21 Electromagnetic induction

Exam questions often require that you demonstrate knowledge from different topics and the connections between them. These are called synoptic questions. You looked at connections between topics in Chapter 4: Turning effects. You need to make sure that you recognise when a question requires such connections to be made and how to demonstrate these in your answers. For example, questions related to this chapter will often also contain material from Chapter 16: Magentism and Chapter 20: Electromagentism, as the topics are closely linked. As you work through the questions in this chapter, see if you can spot the synoptic questions and think carefully about how best to answer them.

21.1 Generating electricity

1   A dynamo is a type of generator. It can be attached to a bicycle wheel in a way that makes the turning of the wheel operate the dynamo. This is used to power a bicycle's lamp.

   a   What are the essential parts of a dynamo?

   b   What needs to happen so that the dynamo generates electricity?

   c   The brightness of the lamp increases when the dynamo's induced e.m.f. increases. List three ways to increase the brightness: one change that the cyclist can make, and two changes to the dynamo itself.

2   Figure 21.1 shows a wire being moved in a magnetic field.
    The wire cuts field lines as it moves.

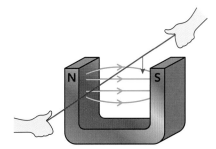

Figure 21.1: Piece of wire being moved in a magnetic field

   a   When the wire is moving, there is a voltage (e.m.f.) across its ends.
       What is the name of this phenomenon?

   b   The ends of the wire are connected to make a complete circuit. What is the name of the rule that shows the direction of the current in the wire, and what does each finger or thumb represent?

   c   What is the direction of the current in the piece of wire?

3   A student sets up an experiment using a coil, a permanent magnet and a galvanometer (a device for measuring very small currents) as shown in Figure 21.2.

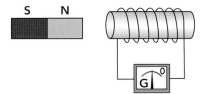

Figure 21.2

   a   The student moves the magnet towards the coil, and while this is happening an e.m.f. is induced across the ends of the coil. Explain why.   [1]

b   While the student moves the magnet towards the coil, the galvanometer
    needle deflects to the right. This shows that a current is flowing through
    the galvanometer from left to right. Explain why the current flows in
    this direction.   [3]

c   Predict what the galvanometer will show in each of the
    following situations:

    i   moving the magnet towards the coil more slowly   [1]

    ii   keeping the magnet stationary next the coil, in the position
         shown in Figure 21.2)   [1]

    iii moving the magnet away from the coil (towards the left).   [1]

d   Predict and explain what the galvanometer shows if the magnet
    is held still and the coil is moved away from it (towards the right).   [2]

[Total: 9]

4   Figure 21.3 shows a simple a.c. generator.

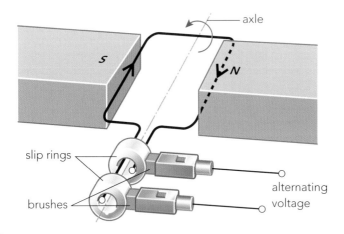

Figure 21.3

a   Explain why slip rings are used.   [2]

b   Explain why the generator produces an alternating voltage instead
    of a constant voltage.   [1]

    A graph of the output voltage (e.m.f.) from the generator is shown
    in Figure 21.4 with four points labelled.

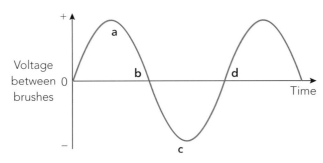

Figure 21.4

c   State and explain whether the coil is horizontal (as shown in Figure 21.3) or vertical at point c on the graph. [3]

d   Explain why the voltage is zero at point d on the graph. [2]

e   The time between points a and b on the graph is 0.02 s. Determine the time taken for one complete rotation of the coil. [1]

[Total: 9]

UNDERSTAND THESE TERMS

- a.c. generator
- electromagnetic induction
- Fleming's right-hand rule
- induced e.m.f.
- Lenz's law
- slip rings

≪ RECALL AND CONNECT 1 ≪

What is the motor effect?

21.2 Power lines and transformers

1   A mobile phone (cell phone) is plugged into a 220 V mains supply to recharge its battery. However, the battery requires a voltage of only 5 V to charge it.

a   The phone's charger contains a transformer that converts 220 V to 5 V. What is the name of this type of transformer?

b   Write, in its simplest form, the ratio of number of turns in the primary coil to the number of turns in the secondary coil of the phone charger's transformer.

c   If the number of turns in the primary coil is 440, what is the number of turns in the secondary coil?

d   The phone uses 5 V d.c., so its charging cable also contains a circuit that converts a.c. to d.c. What is the difference between a.c. and d.c.?

2   a   Draw the circuit symbol for a transformer.

b   Figure 21.5 shows a student's drawing of a step-up transformer. Find two errors in the student's diagram.

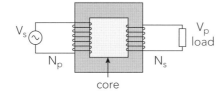

Figure 21.5: Student's drawing of a step-up transformer, with errors

3   A power station supplies power to local industries, homes and shops as shown in Figure 21.6.

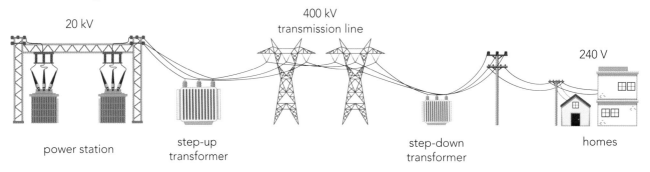

Figure 21.6

a   State and explain one advantage of transmitting electricity at a high voltage. [2]

b   Describe the parts of a simple transformer. [2]

c   State the function of a step-up transformer. [1]

d   If the step-up transformer in Figure 21.6 has 80 000 turns in its secondary coil, calculate the number of turns in its primary coil. [2]

e   Determine the ratio of primary turns to secondary turns in the step-down transformer in Figure 21.6. [1]

f   The diagram shows one step-down transformer, but usually a series of transformers would be used to step down from 400 kV to 240 V. Suggest a reason why. [1]

[Total: 9]

UNDERSTAND THESE TERMS

- national grid
- power lines
- primary coil
- secondary coil
- step-down transformer
- step-up transformer
- transformer

REFLECTION

There are different ways to approach a calculation of voltage or number of turns in a transformer. One way is to use the equation $\dfrac{V_P}{V_S} = \dfrac{N_P}{N_S}$ and rearrange it as necessary. Alternatively, you can write the relationship as $V_P : V_S = N_P : N_S$ substitute the known values and then work out the missing value in one of the ratios. Which method are you most confident with? Do you need to work on your equation rearranging skills?

« RECALL AND CONNECT 2 «

An electric motor runs from the 230 V mains supply. The current flowing through it is 0.5 A. At what rate is electrical energy transferred by the motor? How much energy is transferred in 2 minutes?

21.3 How transformers work

1 Choose from the words in brackets to complete the sentences below.

When electricity is transmitted across long distances, it is more efficient to use (low/high) voltage and (low/high) current. This is because when the (current/voltage) is high, this causes more heating of the wires, which wastes energy. If the power is fixed, the current (halves/doubles) if the voltage doubles.

2 **a** What type of voltage do transformers work with?

b What is the purpose of the core of a transformer?

c What type of material is a transformer core made from, and why?

d Why is energy lost in electrical wires, and what is the equation for calculating the rate of energy loss?

e Under what condition is the equation $I_P V_P = I_S V_S$ true for a transformer?

3 A laptop is connected to a 120 V a.c. mains supply. The laptop's power cable contains a transformer with 600 turns in its primary coil. The output voltage and current of the transformer are 12 V and 1.5 A.

a What is the output power of the transformer?

b If the transformer is 100% efficient, what is the current in the primary coil of the transformer?

c What is the number of turns on the secondary coil of the transformer?

4 A school in a remote area gets its electricity from a small hydroelectric power station, via a step-down transformer. The power station is only used to supply electricity to the school.

The output power and voltage of the power station are 50 kW and 25 kV. The school requires a voltage of 250 V.

a Calculate the current in the cables connecting the power station to the transformer. [2]

b The total resistance in the cables connecting the power station to the transformer is 25 Ω. Calculate the power loss in the cables. [2]

c Suggest two ways to reduce the power loss. [2]

d If the number of turns in the secondary coil of the transformer is 40, calculate the number of turns in the primary coil. [3]

e Calculate the current supplied to the school if the transformer is 100% efficient. (Ignore the effects of power losses in cables.) [2]

[Total: 11]

5 Explain why there is an e.m.f. across the secondary coil of a transformer when there is an e.m.f. across the primary coil. **[Total: 3]**

≪ RECALL AND CONNECT 3 ≪

Write the equations used to calculate *fractional* efficiency in terms of energy and power.

A lamp has an input power of 25 W. It transfers 15 W as light, and 10 W is wasted through heating. Calculate the percentage efficiency of the lamp.

SELF-ASSESSMENT CHECKLIST

Let's revisit the Knowledge focus and Exam skills focus for this chapter.

Decide how confident you are with each statement.

Now I can	Show it	Needs more work	Almost there	Confident to move on
list the factors affecting the size and direction of an e.m.f. induced in a circuit	Describe a way to induce an e.m.f. across a piece of wire, and give three ways to increase the size of the e.m.f.			
describe the structure and use of step-up and stepdown transformers	Draw step-up and step-down transformers and explain the differences between them. Write a calculation question that asks for a voltage or number of turns for a transformer coil. Swap questions with a classmate and answer each other's.			
explain how a transformer works	Explain the operation of a transformer to a friend or family member. Explain what it means for a transformer to be 100% efficient.			
practise answering synoptic questions.	Look through one or more of the Exam practice sections – or some past papers – and circle all the synoptic questions. Make a list of any topics that are commonly covered in the same question.			

Exam practice 5

This section contains past paper questions from previous Cambridge exams, which draws together your knowledge on a range of topics that you have covered up to this point. These questions give you the opportunity to test your knowledge and understanding. Additional past paper practice questions can be found in the accompanying digital material.

The following question has an example student response and commentary provided. Once you have worked through the question, read the student response and commentary. Are your answers different to the sample answers?

1   a   Complete the following sentences.

     i   An electric current exists in a wire when .... are made to flow in the wire.   [1]

     ii   The current in a wire may be measured using an instrument called ....   [1]

     iii   The potential difference across a wire may be measured by connecting .... across the wire.   [1]

  b   A length of resistance wire is connected in a simple series circuit.

    The current in it is 0.8 A. The potential difference across it is 9.6 V.

    Calculate the resistance of the wire.   [4]

  c   The resistance wire in **b** is replaced by a greater length of wire from the same reel.

    Without further calculation, state the effect this has on

     i   the resistance in the circuit

     ii   the current in the new wire when there is a potential difference of 9.6 V across it, as before.   [2]

                                            [Total: 9]

Cambridge IGCSE Physics (0625) Paper 21, Q8, June 2012

Example student response	Commentary
1 **a** **i** electrons	The student's response is correct. (The response 'charges' would also be acceptable). *This answer is awarded 1 out of 1 mark.*
ii a current meter	The student's response is incorrect. This instrument is called an ammeter. *This answer is awarded 0 out of 0 marks.*
iii a voltmeter	The student's response is correct. *This answer is awarded 1 out of 1 mark.*
b $0.8 \times 9.6 = 7.68\ \Omega$	The student's response is incorrect. They have simply multiplied the two quantities given in the question without considering the correct relationship between resistance, current and potential difference, which is $R = \dfrac{V}{I}$. However, they have written the correct unit symbol (representing ohms). *This answer is awarded 1 out of 4 marks.*
c **i** The resistance in the circuit increases because a longer wire has more resistance than a shorter wire.	This response gives the correct effect on the resistance. The explanation is also correct, but the question did not ask for an explanation so this gains no additional marks. There is also no need to repeat part of the question. The much shorter response 'it increases' would have been enough to gain the mark. *This answer is awarded 1 out of 1 mark.*
ii It is the same because it has the same potential difference.	The student's response is incorrect. The potential difference is the same but the resistance is greater, so according to the equation $I = \dfrac{V}{R}$, the current decreases. *This answer is awarded 0 out of 1 mark.*

Now you have read the commentary to the previous question, here is a question on a similar topic which you should attempt. Use the information from the previous response and commentary to guide you as you answer.

2 The power supply used in an electric vehicle contains 990 rechargeable cells each of electromotive force (e.m.f.) 1.2V.

The cells are contained in packs in which all the cells are in series with each other. The e.m.f. of each pack is 54V.

a Calculate the number of packs in the power supply. [2]

b When in use, each pack supplies a current of 3.5A.

    i Calculate the rate at which each cell is transferring chemical energy to electrical energy. [2]

    ii The packs are connected in parallel to supply a large current to drive the electric vehicle.

    Explain why it is necessary to use thick wires to carry this current. [3]

[Total: 7]

Cambridge IGCSE Physics (0625) Paper 41, Q8, June 2020

The following question has an example student commentary and answer provided. Work through the question first, then compare your answer to the sample answer and commentary. Are your answers different to the sample responses? What information does this give you about your understanding of this topic?

3   Figure 3.1 shows a metal kettle used for heating water. The kettle is connected to the mains power supply. The metal case is connected to earth. A fault causes the live wire to come loose and touch the metal case, as shown.

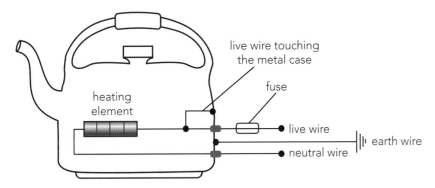

Figure 3.1

a   i   The kettle is switched on. There is a very large electric current in the live wire.

Explain why this large electric current can be dangerous.   [1]

ii   Explain how a fuse helps to protect against the danger of a large electric current.   [2]

iii   Explain why the kettle is **not** safe to use with the fuse connected into the neutral wire instead of the live wire.   [1]

b   The current in a device when operating normally is 3.1A.

State a suitable value for the fuse.

Choose **one** of these values: 3A, 5A, 10A or 13A.   [1]

c   A small kettle has a potential difference (p.d.) of 12V (d.c.) across its heating element. The current in the heating element is 2.5A.

Calculate, in Ω, the resistance of the heating element.   [3]

[Total: 8]

Adapted from *Cambridge IGCSE Physics (0625) Paper 32, Q10, November 2020*

Example student response	Commentary
3 a i It can give you an electric shock.	The student's answer is not correct. If a person touches the kettle they will not get a shock, because current will flow more easily through the earth wire than through the person. The hazard in this situation is overheating which could cause a fire. *This answer is awarded 0 out of 1 mark.*
ii It breaks if the current is too large.	'Melts' would be a better term to use here, but 'breaks' is an acceptable description of how the fuse behaves. The student's response does not explain why it is helpful for the fuse to break: it stops current flowing in the circuit. *This answer is awarded 1 out of 2 marks.*
iii Because it won't break if the current gets too large.	The student's statement is not correct. The current flows in the neutral wire as well as the live wire, so the fuse will still melt if there is a high current. The problem is that the kettle will still be live (connected to the mains at high voltage) even after the fuse melts. *This answer is awarded 0 out of 2 marks.*
b 10 A	The correct choice is the lowest fuse value that is higher than the current needed by the device. That would be 5 A. *This answer is awarded 0 out of 1 mark.*
c 4.8 Ω	The student's response is correct. However, it is not a good habit to write the answer without the formula or calculation (which would be: $R = V \div I = 12 \div 2.5$). If the student had done the division incorrectly, or copied the answer incorrectly from their calculator, they would have gained no marks at all because they did not show any correct steps. It is also more difficult for the student to check their calculation afterwards when they have only written down the final answer. *This answer is awarded 3 out of 3 marks.*

Now you have read the commentary to the previous question, here is a question on a similar topic which you should attempt. Use the information from the previous response and commentary to guide you as you answer.

4 **a** Figure 4.1 shows a simple circuit.

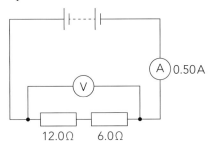

Figure 4.1

   i The current in the wires of the circuit is a flow of particles.
       Indicate the name of these particles. Tick **one** box.

   ☐ electrons

   ☐ atoms

   ☐ protons   [1]

   ii Calculate, in Ω, the combined resistance of the two resistors.   [1]

   iii Calculate, in V, the potential difference (p.d.) reading that would
        be shown on the voltmeter.   [3]

b The circuit is changed.

   The two resistors are connected in parallel.

   Explain what happens, if anything, to the current reading on the ammeter.   [2]

                                                                        [Total: 7]

Adapted from *Cambridge IGCSE Physics (0625) Paper 32, Q9, June 2018*

The following question has an example student response and commentary provided. Once you have worked through the question, read the student response and commentary. Are your answers different to the sample answers?

5 **a** Figure 5.1 shows the cross-section of a wire carrying a current into the plane of the paper.

       On Figure. 5.1, sketch the magnetic field due to the current in the wire.
       The detail of your sketch should suggest the variation in the strength
       of the field. Show the direction of the field with arrows.   [3]

Figure 5.1

b Figure 5.2 shows part of a model of a d.c. motor.

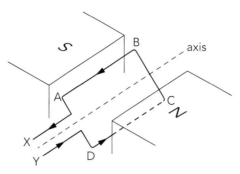

Figure 5.2

A loop of wire ABCD is placed between the poles of a magnet. The loop is free to rotate about the axis shown. There is a current in the loop in the direction indicated by the arrows.

i On Figure 5.2, draw arrows to show the directions of the forces acting on side AB and on side CD of the loop. [1]

ii With the loop in the position shown in Figure 5.2, explain why the forces on AB and CD cause the loop to rotate about the axis. [1]

iii The ends X and Y of the loop are connected to a battery using brushes and a split-ring commutator.

State why a split-ring commutator is used. [2]

[Total: 7]

Cambridge IGCSE Physics (0625) Paper 31, Q10, June 2013

Example student response	Commentary
5 a ⊗	The student's sketch correctly shows that the field lines are circular and centred on the wire. The arrow also shows the correct direction. (It would be better to draw an arrow on each field line, but one arrow is enough to gain the mark for showing direction.) However, the spacing of the circles should increase as the radius increases, to show that the field strength decreases with distance from the wire. *This answer is awarded 2 out of 3 marks*
b i [Student draws an arrow on side AB pointing up and an arrow on side CD pointing down.].	This response is incorrect, as the force on side AB is downwards and the force on side CD is upwards. The left-hand rule should be used to determine these directions correctly. *This answer is awarded 0 out of 1 mark.*
ii The forces are at a distance from the pivot (which is the axis), so they cause moments (turning effects).	The student has made a statement that is correct but has not fully explained why the coil rotates. The answer needs to mention that the two moments cause rotation because they are both in the same direction (so they do not cancel out). *This answer is awarded 0 out of 1 mark.*

Example student response	Commentary
iii It lets the coil rotate without getting twisted, and makes sure the coil always rotates in the same direction.	This response includes the essential point that it makes sure the rotation is always in the same direction. The student has not mentioned that the commutator does this by reversing the current in the loop every half turn. *This answer is awarded 1 out of 2 marks.*

Now you have read the commentary to the previous question, here is a question on a similar topic which you should attempt. Use the information from the previous response and commentary to guide you as you answer.

6   Figure 6.1 shows a horizontal wire PQ placed in the gap between the N pole and the S pole of a magnet.

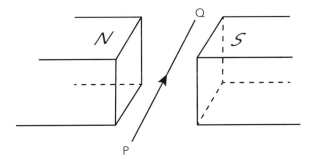

Figure 6.1

There is a current in the wire in the direction P to Q.

A force acts on the current-carrying wire in the magnetic field.

a   On Figure 6.1, draw:

    i   an arrow, labelled M to show the direction of the magnetic field in the gap between the poles of the magnet   [1]

    ii   an arrow, labelled F to show the direction of the force on the current-carrying wire due to the magnetic field of the magnet.   [1]

b   State the effect of reversing the direction of the current in wire PQ.   [1]

c   The magnet is removed and the horizontal, current-carrying wire is left on its own, as shown in Figure 6.2.

    i   On Figure 6.2, sketch the pattern of the magnetic field due to the current in the wire.

    Indicate the field direction.   [3]

    ii   The current in PQ is **increased**.

    State the effect of this change in current on the magnetic field.   [1]

d   A small magnet is placed at a point where the magnetic field is vertically upwards. State the direction of the force on the S pole of the small magnet.   [1]

[Total: 8]

Q

P

Figure 6.2

Cambridge IGCSE Physics (0625) Paper 42, Q9, June 2017

The following question has an example student response and commentary provided. Once you have worked through the question, read the student response and commentary. Are your answers different to the sample answers?

7 A radio is connected to the mains supply using a step-down transformer.

   a Draw a labelled diagram of the structure of a basic step-down transformer. [3]

   b Explain the operation of a basic transformer. [3]

   c The voltage of the mains supply is 230V. The output voltage of the transformer is 6.0V.

   Calculate the value of the turns ratio $\left(\dfrac{N_S}{N_P}\right)$. Give your answer to two significant figures. [2]

   [Total: 8]

Cambridge IGCSE Physics (0625) Paper 42, Q8, March 2022

Example student response	Commentary
7 a core	The student's diagram is partly correct: it shows a core and two correctly labelled coils. However, the secondary coil (on the right) should have fewer turns than the primary coil because this is a step-down transformer. *This answer is awarded 2 out of 3 marks.*
b A current in the primary coil produces a changing magnetic field around the secondary coil. This induces an e.m.f. in the secondary coil.	The student's response is correct but incomplete. The term 'alternating current' should be used, as this is essential to the working of a transformer. *This answer is awarded 2 out of 3 marks.*
c $\dfrac{230}{6} = 57.5$	The student's response is incorrect. The correct equation is $\dfrac{N_s}{N_P} = \dfrac{V_s}{V_P}$. Therefore $\dfrac{N_s}{N_P} = \dfrac{6}{230} \approx 0.026$. *This answer is awarded 0 out of 2 marks.*

Now you have read the commentary to the previous question, here is a question on a similar topic which you should attempt. Use the information from the previous response and commentary to guide you as you answer.

8   Figure 8.1 shows a permanent bar magnet next to a circuit that contains a coil and a galvanometer.

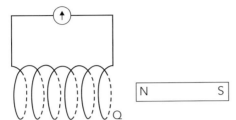

Figure 8.1

a   Suggest a metal from which the magnet is made.   [1]

b   The magnet is moved to the left and inserted a small distance into the coil. The galvanometer deflects briefly and shows that there is current in the coil.

   i   Explain why there is a current in the coil.   [2]

   ii   As the magnet is moving near to the coil, end Q of the coil behaves as a magnetic pole.

        State the polarity of end Q and explain why it has this polarity.   [2]

c   Suggest **two** ways in which the deflection of the galvanometer can be reversed.   [2]

[Total: 7]

Cambridge IGCSE Physics (0625) Paper 42, Q9, November 2018

22 The nuclear atom

KNOWLEDGE FOCUS

In this chapter, you will answer questions on:

- atomic structure
- protons, neutrons and electrons.

EXAM SKILLS FOCUS

In this chapter you will:

- continue to think about your own learning and the revision strategies that work best for you.

As you work through the questions in this chapter think back to the different learning strategies that you have been introduced to throughout this book. Which strategies work best for your ways of learning?

Continue using the reflection features and self-assessment checklist at the end of the chapter to help you reflect on your learning.

Further support is available in the exam skills chapter at the start of this book.

22.1 Atomic structure

1 a What is the 'solar system model' (sometimes called the planetary model or Rutherford model) of the atom?

In a chemical reaction, an atom of aluminium reacts with three atoms of chlorine. During the reaction, the aluminium atom loses three electrons and each chlorine atom gains one electron.

  b Is the aluminium positively or negatively charged after the electron transfer?

  c Is the chlorine positively or negatively charged after the electron transfer?

  d What is the term used for the process by which ions are formed?

2 The physicists Geiger and Marsden carried out an experiment in which they fired particles at a very thin piece of gold foil.

  a The experiment was carried out in a vacuum. Explain why. [1]

  b Before this experiment, the plum pudding model of the atom was widely used by physicists. In the plum pudding model, the positive charge of an atom is spread out throughout its volume.

Scientists were expecting all the alpha particles to pass straight through the foil. Use the plum pudding model to suggest why. [1]

  c Explain how the observations made in this experiment led to the nuclear model of the atom. [4]

[Total: 6]

REFLECTION

A successful answer to Question 2 depends on both knowledge and understanding. Can you visualise or describe the alpha scattering experiment setup and observations? If not, you may find it difficult to understand and recall the experiment well. You can use your textbook or find images, simulations or videos about this experiment online – what would be most effective for helping you understand and remember it? How could you find websites where the explanations are at a level suitable for IGCSE students?

UNDERSTAND THESE TERMS

- alpha particle
- ionisation
- nucleus
- plum pudding model

≪ RECALL AND CONNECT 1 ≪

What is electromagnetic induction? What is the useful energy transfer that occurs in a generator?

22.2 Protons, neutrons and electrons

1 For a nucleus with nuclide notation $_Z^A X$, what is:

   a the relative charge

   b the relative mass?

2 A nuclear reaction can be represented by the following equation (where H represents hydrogen and He represents helium):

$$_1^2\text{H} + \,_2^3\text{H} \rightarrow \,_2^4\text{He} + \,_0^1\text{n} + \text{energy}$$

   a What is the difference between fission and fusion? Does the equation above represent a nuclear fusion or a nuclear fission reaction?

   b What particle does the symbol $_0^1\text{n}$ represent, and what are its relative charge and relative mass?

   c What is the relationship between the numbers on the two sides of the equation, and why?

3 a The element chlorine has two common isotopes, $_{17}^{35}\text{Cl}$ and $_{17}^{37}\text{Cl}$. Define the term 'isotopes'. [1]

   b Compare the numbers of each type of particle in neutral atoms of $_{17}^{35}\text{Cl}$ and $_{17}^{37}\text{Cl}$. [3]

   c An isotope of nitrogen has 8 neutrons. Its neutral atom has 7 electrons. Write the nuclide notation for this isotope. (The symbol for nitrogen is N.) [2]

   d A different isotope of nitrogen has mass number 14. State the number of neutrons in its atom. Explain your answer. [2]

   [Total: 8]

4 A nucleus of the element plutonium is hit by a neutron. The equation below summarises what happens:

$$_{94}^{239}\text{Pu} + \,_0^1\text{n} \rightarrow \,_p^{96}\text{Sr} + \,_{56}^q\text{Ba} + 4\,_0^1\text{n} + \text{energy}$$

   a Determine the missing numbers p and q in the equation. [2]

   b Name the type of reaction represented by the equation. [1]

   c Explain how energy is released in this type of reaction. [1]

   [Total: 4]

≪ RECALL AND CONNECT 2 ≪

What are the main parts of a transformer? What type of current is needed in the primary coil for a transformer to work? What effects do step-up and step-down transformers have on current and voltage?

UNDERSTAND THESE TERMS
- neutron
- neutron number
- nucleon
- nucleon number
- proton
- proton number
- relative mass

UNDERSTAND THESE TERMS
- isotope
- relative charge
- relative mass

REFLECTION

Could you answer all the questions in this chapter? If there was a question you answered incorrectly, was it because: you did not understand the topic fully; you could not recall a key term or other piece of knowledge; or because you had the required knowledge and understanding but misunderstood a question or did not answer fully enough? What, if anything, do you need to do to improve in this topic?

SELF-ASSESSMENT CHECKLIST

Let's revisit the Knowledge focus and Exam skills focus for this chapter.

Decide how confident you are with each statement.

Now I can	Show it	Needs more work	Almost there	Confident to move on
describe the structure of the atom	Draw and label a diagram to show the particles in an atom.			
represent nuclei in the form $^A_Z X$	List the properties of the particles in atomic nuclei. Explain to a friend or family member the meaning of the notation $^A_Z X$.			
explain what isotopes are	Describe similarities and differences between two isotopes of an element.			
name and state the mass and charge of the particles in the nucleus	List the proton number, nucleon number, mass and charge of any element in the Periodic Table.			
continue to think about your own learning and the revision strategies that work best for you.	Make a list of the different learning strategies you have been introduced to in this book. Discuss the differences between these with a friend.			

23 Radioactivity

KNOWLEDGE FOCUS

In this chapter, you will answer questions on:

- radioactivity all around us
- radioactive decay
- activity and half-life

 using radioisotopes.

EXAM SKILLS FOCUS

In this chapter you will:

- show that you understand the command word 'deduce' and can answer 'deduce' questions.

In this chapter you will answer questions containing the command word 'deduce'.

Deduce	conclude from available information.

This command word is typically used when you need to come to a decision based on information given in the question, such as a data table or graph. As part of a 'deduce' question, you will often be asked to justify or explain your decision. Remember to answer both parts – that is, write down what you deduce, and then explain or justify it.

23.1 Radioactivity all around us

1 Background radiation can be classed as natural or artificial.

   a What is the difference between artificial background radiation and natural background radiation?

   b Categorise each of the following as sources of natural background radiation or artificial radiation.

> X-ray imaging   food and drink   cosmic rays
> nuclear energy industry   buildings and soil   radon gas

   c Why are X-rays included in background radiation even though X-rays are not caused by radioactive decay?

   d What is the difference between contamination by a radioactive source and irradiation by a radioactive source?

2 Fresh fruit can be made to last longer by exposure to nuclear radiation, which kills living cells including bacteria. This process is called irradiation.

A worker uses a Geiger counter to measure the count rate next to some apples that have just been irradiated.

   a Define the term 'count rate'. [1]

   b Explain why the count rate next to the apples is **not** higher after the irradiation than before. [1]

   c The average count rate measured anywhere on Earth is not zero. Explain why. [1]

   d Average count rates measured at high altitudes (far above sea level) are typically higher than at low altitudes. Explain why. [1]

[Total: 4]

≪ RECALL AND CONNECT 1 ≪

One of the isotopes of the element boron is written in nuclide notation as $^{11}_{5}B$. Make a list of everything that this notation tells you about this isotope. What would be the nuclide notation for an isotope of boron with one less neutron in its atom?

UNDERSTAND THESE TERMS

- background radiation
- contaminated
- count rate
- irradiated
- radiation
- radioactive substance

23.2 Radioactive decay

1 **a** Nuclear radiation is described as random and spontaneous.
What does each of these terms mean?

b Which types of radioactive decay cause a nucleus of an element to change into a nucleus of a different element?

c What are the symbols for alpha, beta and gamma radiation?

d What are alpha particles, beta particles and gamma rays composed of?

2 **a** Which of the three types of radiation is the most penetrating?

b Give a type of barrier that is usually effective for blocking or mostly blocking:

i alpha radiation

ii beta radiation

iii gamma radiation.

c What is ionisation?

d Which of the three types of radiation is the most ionising?

3 **a** How do alpha, beta and gamma particles behave in electric fields?

b Which rule can be used to predict the directions of the forces on nuclear radiation in a magnetic field? Which way should the second finger point for alpha particles and for beta particles?

4 **a** List two possible reasons for a nucleus to be unstable.

b During beta emission, which particle in the nucleus changes, and what does it change into?

c Write an equation for the beta decay of the nucleus $^A_Z Q$ into a nucleus of element R. Use the symbol β for a beta particle and write it using nuclide notation.

5 Some cancerous tumours are treated by inserting a small metal rod, about the size of a grain of rice, into or next to the tumour. Inside the metal rod is a radioactive isotope.

This technique can be used to treat tumours that are up to a few millimetres thick.

a State which type of emitter (alpha, beta or gamma) would be most suitable, and justify your choice. [3]

b Give one reason why exposure to nuclear radiation can be harmful to living organisms. [1]

c   The radioactive source may be left in place for several days. During this time, the patient stays in hospital in a separate room from other patients. If the patient has visitors, the visitors are only allowed to stay for a limited time.

Suggest why it is considered appropriate for the patient to be exposed to the radiation for several days, yet visitors must only stay for short periods. [1]

d   Give three safety precautions that should be taken by people who work with radioactive sources. [3]

[Total: 8]

6   An unstable nucleus of element X decays into a nucleus of element Y as shown in the equation below:

$$^{p}_{84}X \rightarrow\, ^{210}_{q}Y + \alpha$$

a   Rewrite the alpha particle symbol using nuclide notation. [2]

b   Determine the value of p in the equation. [1]

c   Determine the value of q in the equation. [1]

d   The nucleus of element Y then decays into a nucleus of element Z by beta decay. Write an equation for this decay. [3]

e   The nucleus of Z emits a gamma ray. Explain why a nucleus undergoes gamma decay. [1]

f   Beta radiation is less strongly ionising than alpha radiation. Give two reasons why. [2]

[Total: 10]

UNDERSTAND THESE TERMS
• alpha decay
• beta decay
• beta particle
• gamma ray
• ionising nuclear radiation
• radioactive decay
• radioisotope
• random process

REFLECTION

The mark scheme for Question 5a shows several possible ways to gain the marks. Read all of these and think about why they are acceptable answers. Note that you do not have to say everything in the mark scheme to be awarded full marks. If you did not gain full marks for this question, can you see how to improve your answer?

23.3 Activity and half-life

1   Tritium is a radioactive isotope of hydrogen.

a   Tritium has a half-life of 12.3 years. What does this mean?

b   A sample contains 1000 mg of tritium. Find the mass of tritium remaining after 24.6 years.

c   Work out how long it would take for 800 mg of tritium to reduce to 50 mg.

2 How are source count rate measurements corrected for background radiation?

3 Carbon-14 has a half-life of 5730 years.

   a Define 'half-life'. [1]

   b Predict the mass of carbon-14 remaining in a pure sample of mass 80 g after 5 half-lives. [2]

   c A sample contains 100 g of carbon-14. Determine the time taken for the mass of carbon-14 to fall to 12.5 g. [2]

   d Suggest why this method could not be used to make an accurate measurement of the age of a object that is 500 000 years old. [2]

[Total: 7]

4 The graph in Figure 23.1 shows how the count rate of a radioactive isotope sample changes over time.

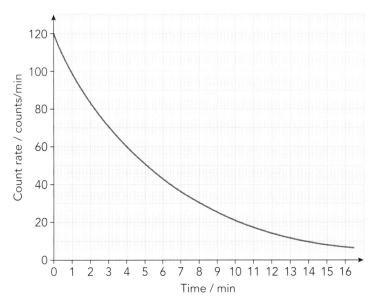

Figure 23.1

   a Determine the half-life of this isotope. [1]

   b Determine how many minutes it took for the count rate to decrease by 75%. [2]

   c Predict the count rate 18 minutes after the starting time. [2]

[Total: 5]

UNDERSTAND THESE TERMS
• activity
• half-life

23.4 Using radioisotopes

1 a i   Why can nuclear radiation be used to sterilise medical equipment?

ii   Which type of radiation is used to sterilise medical equipment?

b i   What is a radioactive tracer?

ii   Give two uses of radioactive tracers.

2   Most radioactive isotopes emit more than one type of radiation. However, there are some isotopes that emit radiation that is all, or almost all, of only one type. The table shows information about six of these.

Radioactive isotope	Half-life	Type of radiation emitted	
polonium-210	140 days	alpha	
plutonium-238	88 years	alpha	
krypton-85	11 years	beta	
lead-209	3.3 hours	beta	
cobalt-60	5.3 years	gamma	
technetium-99m	6.0 hours	gamma	

a   Using information in the table, deduce which of the isotopes would be most suitable for monitoring the thickness of aluminium foil (kitchen foil) being produced in a factory. Explain your choice.   [3]

b   Using information in the table, deduce which of the isotopes would be most suitable for use as a tracer in medicine. Explain your choice.   [4]

c   A pacemaker is a small electrical device implanted into a person's heart to correct an irregular heartbeat.

i   Radioactive decay releases energy. In the past, a small amount of radioactive material was used as the power supply for a pacemaker. Using information in the table, state which of the isotopes would have been most suitable for this use. Justify your choice.   [4]

ii   Pacemakers are now powered using a battery instead of a radioactive source. The battery must be replaced every five to ten years. Suggest one reason why batteries are now used in pacemakers instead of radioactive sources.   [1]

[Total: 12]

> **UNDERSTAND THESE TERMS**
>
> • radioactive tracing
> • radiocarbon dating

≪ RECALL AND CONNECT 2 ≪

In what ways did the alpha scattering experiment change physicists' model of the atom?

SELF-ASSESSMENT CHECKLIST

Let's revisit the Knowledge focus and Exam skills focus for this chapter.

Decide how confident you are with each statement.

Now I can	Show it	Needs more work	Almost there	Confident to move on
explain the term 'background radiation' and list some of its sources	List the main sources of background radiation and classify each one as natural or artificial.			
describe radioactive decay	Plan how you would teach the concept of radioactive decay, including its random and spontaneous behaviour, to someone who knows the structure of an atom but does not know what nuclear decay is.			
define and calculate radioactive half-life	For 16 000 atoms of a radioactive isotope with a half-life of 10 minutes, make a table showing the expected number of atoms remaining every 10 minutes up to an hour. Sketch a graph of number of atoms remaining against time.			
use radioisotopes	Recall at least one use of each of alpha, beta and gamma radiations. In each case, say why that type of radiation is the best choice for that use, and suggest a suitable half-life, with an explanation.			
show that I understand the command word 'deduce' and can answer 'deduce' questions.	Write an exam-style question using the command word 'deduce' in which students are asked to choose one of the three types of nuclear radiation and explain why it is the best choice. Ask a classmate to answer your question and mark their response. Explain why you awarded that number of marks.			

24 Earth and the Solar System

Many questions ask you to compare two or more things, or list similarities and differences. The instructional text in the question will sometimes specify what is expected of you. It is important to ensure you use comparatives (such as 'larger', 'weaker', 'more likely' and so on) when answering such questions and do not simply describe individual characteristics.

Compare	identify/comment on similarities and/or differences.

24.1 Earth, Sun and Moon

1 Decide whether each of the statements below is true or false.

  a The Earth's rotation causes seasons and the Earth's orbit causes day and night.

  b The Earth is closer to the Sun in summer and farther from the Sun in winter.

  c When the days are longer than the nights in the southern hemisphere, the nights are longer than the days in the northern hemisphere.

  d For an observer standing at the north pole, the length of the day does not change during the year.

  e When the Moon is not full, it is because part of it is in the Earth's shadow.

  f When the northern hemisphere experiences a new Moon, the southern hemisphere experiences a full Moon.

2 Figure 24.1 shows sunlight hitting the Earth.

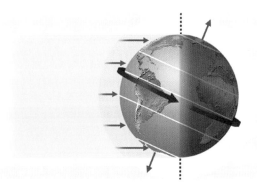

Figure 24.1

  a Explain why an observer on Earth experiences day and night. [2]

  b State and explain the length of the day in the south pole at the time of year shown in Figure 24.1. [2]

  c State and explain which season the northern hemisphere is experiencing in Figure 24.1. [2]

  d Explain why the Earth has seasons. [2]

  e **i** Give the name of the line around the Earth on which the day length is the same all year. [1]

  ii State the length of a day on this line. [1]

[Total: 10]

3   Figure 24.2 shows phases of the Moon as viewed from Earth.

Figure 24.2

a   State the time taken for the Moon to orbit the Earth once.   [1]

b   Explain why we see light from the Moon.   [1]

c   Describe, in words or by sketching, the relative positions of the
     Earth, Moon and Sun when there is a new Moon.   [1]

d   Give the name of the phase of the Moon between new Moon
     and half Moon.   [1]

e   From Earth, we only ever see one side of the Moon. Suggest why.   [1]

[Total: 5]

**UNDERSTAND
THESE TERMS**

- axis
- equator
- hemisphere
- orbit
- phases of the
  Moon

≪ RECALL AND CONNECT 1 ≪

What is the difference between mass and weight?
What is the weight of a person of mass 70 kg on Earth?

24.2 The Solar System

1 Figure 24.3 shows a simplified picture of the Solar System.

Figure 24.3: Gravitational pull of the Sun on objects

a Give two ways in which the representation of the Solar System in Figure 24.3 is correct.

b Give two ways in which the representation of the Solar System in Figure 24.3 is incorrect.

c What keeps the planets in their orbits?

d Which of the planets in the Solar System are rocky?

e Pluto is not categorised as a planet. What type of object is it?

f What is an asteroid?

g What is a comet?

2 Before the planets formed, the Solar System was a spinning disc of gas and dust.

a Over time, disc material started to form into the Sun and planets. Explain why. [1]

b Four of the planets are described as gaseous. State whether these formed in the inner or outer region of the Solar System, and explain why. [2]

c Compare the gravitational field strengths at the surface of Saturn and at the surface of Mercury, and explain why they are different. [2]

d Saturn is approximately 1.4×10^9 km from the Sun. Calculate the time taken for light from the Sun to reach Saturn. Write your answer in minutes. (The speed of light is 3.0×10^8 m/s.) [4]

[Total: 9]

3 The table shows data about four planets.

Planet	Orbital distance / million km	Orbital duration / years	Density / kg/m³	Surface temperature / °C	Gravitational field strength at the surface of the planet / N/kg
Mercury	58	0.2	5500	−18 to 460	4
Earth	150	1	5500	−8 to 58	10
Saturn	1427	30	700	−140	11
Neptune	4497	165	1700	−220	12

a   Explain the variation in surface temperatures of the planets in the table.   [1]

b   Explain why the gravitational field strength on Saturn is greater than on Earth.   [1]

c   Calculate the weight of a person of mass 50 kg standing on the surface of Mercury. Write an appropriate unit with your answer.   [3]

d   Calculate the orbital speed of Neptune, in kilometres per second.   [3]

e   Describe the shape of a comet's orbit.   [1]

f   A comet travels faster when it is closer to the Sun. Explain why, using the concept of energy.   [3]

[Total: 12]

≪ RECALL AND CONNECT 2 ≪

What are alpha, beta and gamma radiation composed of? Compare the ionising and penetrating abilities of these three types of nuclear radiation.

REFLECTION

What are your strengths and weakness on this topic? Past exam papers from before 2023 do not include questions on space physics. How will you make sure you are confident about answering exam questions on this topic?

UNDERSTAND THESE TERMS

- accretion
- accretion disc
- asteroids and meteoroids
- comet
- eccentricity
- ellipse
- minor planet
- orbital period
- orbital radius
- planet

SELF-ASSESSMENT CHECKLIST

Let's revisit the Knowledge focus and Exam skills focus for this chapter.

Decide how confident you are with each statement.

Now I can	Show it	Needs more work	Almost there	Confident to move on
describe the orbital motions of the Earth and Moon and relate these to our measures of time	Explain why Earth has day and night, and seasons.			
describe the eight planets in our Solar System in terms of the formation, movement and satellites	Describe briefly how the Solar System formed. List the planets in order, and describe the nature and location of other objects in the Solar System.			
describe and calculate orbital speed	Solve numerical on finding orbital speed using the key equation $v = 2\pi\dfrac{r}{t}$			
interpret data about orbits and physical properties of planets	Analyse data about orbits and physical properties of planets from table and record accurate responses.			
show that you understand how to make comparisons.	Work through all the questions that ask you to compare two things; look to see how many marks they are worth and check your answers against the mark scheme.			

25 Stars and the Universe

When responding to questions, you will need to judge whether your answer needs to be short, detailed, or structured, if you need to include calculations, or if you need to include specific units. Understanding what is a good answer is very important for questions on this topic. Mark schemes contain a lot of useful information that can teach you how to improve your answers in future. By practising exam-style questions and past paper questions and using the mark schemes to check your responses, you will increasingly recognise what a successful answer looks like. Apart from questions that require you to write a specific scientific term (such as 'electron'), your answers do not have to use exactly the same words as the mark scheme; if your answer clearly has the same meaning, then it is acceptable.

If you can think of several points you could make in the answer to a question, focus on those that you think are most relevant and important – the key ideas rather than the smaller details. Pay attention to the number of marks so that you do not spend too much time giving more detail than is necessary. In this chapter, write down your answers to the questions, mark them and keep them; you will be prompted to look at them again at the end of the chapter.

25.1 The Sun

1   a   Which two elements does the Sun mainly consist of?

    b   In which three regions of the electromagnetic spectrum does the Sun radiate most of its energy?

    c   What is meant by the 'habitable zone' of the Solar System?

2   The equation shows a nuclear reaction that happens within the Sun:

$$^{2}_{1}H + ^{1}_{1}H \rightarrow ^{3}_{2}He$$

    a   State the type of nuclear reaction the reaction shows and explain how you know.   [2]

    b   The reaction releases energy. Give the form of this energy.   [1]

    c   Define 'plasma' and explain why matter inside the Sun is in the plasma state.   [2]

    d   The Sun is described as a 'stable' star. Explain what this means. [1]

                                                                    [Total: 6]

≪ RECALL AND CONNECT 1 ≪

Make a sketch showing how the phases of the Moon are related to the positions of the Moon and Earth relative to the Sun. At each position, show how the Moon looks from Earth, and name the phase.

UNDERSTAND THESE TERMS

- plasma
- solar mass
- stable star

25.2 Stars and galaxies

1   The star Mintaka, in the constellation of Orion, can be seen from almost anywhere on Earth. The distance to Mintaka from Earth has been measured as 1239 light-years.

    a   Is a light-year a unit of speed, distance or time?

    b   A person looks at Mintaka in the year 2025. When did the light they are observing leave the star?

    c   Order these distances from smallest to largest: distances between stars in the Milky Way; distances between galaxies; distances between planets in the Solar System.

2   Name each stage in the life of:

    a   a star of the same mass as the Sun

    b   one of the most massive stars.

3 a Give the name of our galaxy. [1]

   b One of the numbers listed below is the approximate number of stars
      in our galaxy. Circle the correct number. [1]

      10^3 .... 10^5 .... 10^8 .... 10^{11} .... 10^{14}

   c The Andromeda Galaxy is the nearest galaxy to our own. One of the
      numbers listed below is the approximate number of light-years between
      our galaxy and the Andromeda Galaxy. Circle the correct number. [1]

      2.5   25   2500   2.5 million

   d Suggest what causes stars to stay together in a galaxy. [1]

                                                            [Total: 4]

4 Figure 25.1 shows the life cycle of a star.

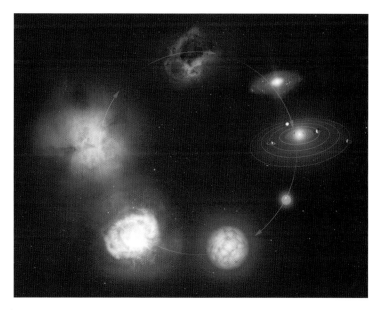

Figure 25.1

   a Describe how the protostar forms. [3]
   b Explain why the star is stable for a period of time. [3]
   c State what causes the star to expand and become a red giant. [1]
   d In the next stage, the outer shell of the red giant is blown away,
      leaving behind a core.
      i   Give the name of the remaining core of the star. [1]
      ii After enough time has passed, the core will no longer emit
          visible light. Explain why. [1]
   e Suggest why Figure 25.1 shows that the life cycle continues after
      the star 'dies'. [1]

                                                            [Total: 10]

5 Proxima Centauri, the nearest star to the Sun, is 4.2 light-years away from Earth.

   a Calculate the distance to Proxima Centauri in metres. [2]

   b The Voyager 1 spacecraft, launched in 1977, has travelled further from Earth than any other object made by humans. It is travelling away from the Sun at a rate of 17 000 m/s.

     Calculate the time it would take, in years, for Voyager to travel from the Sun to Proxima Centauri at this speed. (There are approximately 31 540 000 s in 1 year.) [3]

   c The mass of Proxima Centauri is 0.12 solar masses. Describe the stages of this star's life cycle after most of its hydrogen has been converted to helium. [3]

[Total: 8]

‹‹ RECALL AND CONNECT 2 ‹‹

In which direction must a force act to make an object move in a circular path? How does circular motion change if: the force increases, with the mass and radius remaining constant? If two objects of different mass move in circles, and the radius and speed are the same for both, compare the forces on the two objects.

UNDERSTAND THESE TERMS

- black hole cloud
- interstellar cloud
- light-year
- main sequence
- molecular cloud
- neutron star
- planetary nebula
- protostar
- radiation pressure
- red giant
- red supergiant
- supernova
- white dwarf

25.3 The Universe

1 **a** Which of the following best describes the number of galaxies in the known Universe?

hundreds	thousands	millions	billions

   b What is the approximate diameter of the Milky Way in light-years?

   c What is the Big Bang Theory?

2 **a** What is the CMBR?

   b In what way has the CMBR changed over time?

3 **a** How are the speeds at which galaxies are moving away from Earth measured?

   b Give one way in which distances to far galaxies are determined.

   c What is the Hubble constant, and what is the current estimate of its value, using the unit 'per second'?

4 **a** Define 'redshift'. [2]

   b Describe the relationship between redshift and distance from Earth, for distant galaxies. [1]

   c Tick boxes for all of the ideas below that are supported by observations of redshift. [2]

      A The Universe had a beginning.

      B There are billions of galaxies in the Universe.

      C The Universe is expanding.

      D Distant galaxies are moving away from the Earth.

[Total: 5]

5 Figure 25.2 shows the speeds at which 'superclusters' of galaxies are travelling away from Earth. Clusters are groups of galaxies that are relatively close together, and superclusters are groups of clusters. [2]

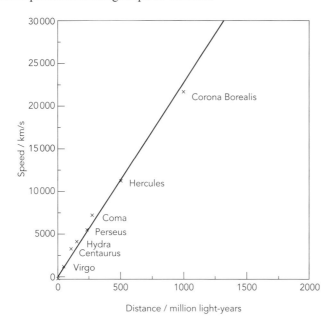

Figure 25.2

   a The graph passes through the origin and through the coordinates (1000, 23 000). Use this fact to calculate the Hubble constant with unit 'per second'. (You will need to use the distance in km.) [4]

   b Determine an estimate for the age of the Universe, in seconds, using the value of Hubble constant calculated in part **a**. [1]

   c Calculate the age of the Universe in years, using the result from part **b**. [1]

   d State and explain which of the superclusters named on the graph has the most redshifted light, when observed from Earth. [2]

   e Explain why redshift observations support the Big Bang theory. [2]

[Total: 10]

> **UNDERSTAND THESE TERMS**
>
> - absorption spectrum
> - Big Bang theory
> - Hubble constant
> - Hubble time
> - Hubble's law
> - redshift

REFLECTION

Did you write down and mark your answers to the Exam skills questions in this chapter? Look at any questions where you did not gain full marks. What can you learn from the mark scheme about how to improve? Even where you gained full marks on a question, you may be able to improve your exam technique by comparing your answers with the mark scheme. Did you include an unnecessary amount of detail, or make statements that were not relevant to the question?

SELF-ASSESSMENT CHECKLIST

Let's revisit the Knowledge focus and Exam skills focus for this chapter.

Decide how confident you are with each statement.

Now I can	Show it	Needs more work	Almost there	Confident to move on
describe the Sun and galaxies, including the Milky Way	State the two elements that the Sun is mostly made of, and the three main types of electromagnetic radiation it emits. State the meaning of a light-year and its value in metres.			
understand the relative separation of planets, stars and galaxies	Imagine how you would teach a younger student about stars and galaxies and help them compare the distances from Earth to other stars in our Solar System, to nearby stars in our galaxy, and to other galaxies.			
recall that the redshift of light from distant galaxies supports the Big Bang theory	Define 'redshift' and 'Big Bang theory' and briefly state how the two are related.			
recognise good quality answers to questions.	In a pair or group, share any tips and techniques you have learned on how to write successful answers to exam questions based on understanding the mark scheme.			

Exam practice 6

This section contains past paper questions from previous Cambridge exams, which draws together your knowledge on a range of topics that you have covered up to this point. These questions give you the opportunity to test your knowledge and understanding. Additional past paper practice questions can be found in the accompanying digital material.

The following answer has an example student response and commentary provided. Once you have worked through the question, read the student response and commentary. Are your answers different to the sample answers?

1 a   An atom of carbon contains protons, neutrons and electrons.

Indicate where each particle is found in the atom. Place a tick in the appropriate box.

particle	in the nucleus	orbiting the nucleus
electron		
neutron		
proton		

[3]

b   An atom of carbon contains 6 protons, 7 neutrons and 6 electrons.

   i   State the proton number of the carbon. [1]

   ii   State the nucleon number of the carbon. [1]

c   Carbon has many different isotopes.

   i   Explain the meaning of the term *isotope*. [2]

   ii   The nuclide notation for the carbon in **b** is $^{13}_{6}\text{C}$.

     Suggest the nuclide notation for another possible isotope of carbon. [1]

[Total: 8]

Cambridge IGCSE Physics (0625) Paper 32, Question 8, November 2017

Example student response	Commentary
1 a electron – orbiting the nucleus neutron – in the nucleus proton – in the nucleus	The student's response is correct. *This answer is awarded 3 out of 3 marks.*
b i 6	The student's response is correct – the proton number is simply the number of protons in the atom. *This answer is awarded 1 out of 1 mark.*
ii 7	The student's response is incorrect. There are 7 *neutrons* in the atom, but the nucleon number is the number of protons and neutrons altogether. *This answer is awarded 0 out of 1 mark.*

Example student response	Commentary
c i An isotope is an atom that has the same number of electrons as another atom.	Isotopes are different atoms of the same element. Atoms can gain or lose electrons while still belonging to the same element, so the number of electrons is not used in the definition of an isotope. To gain the marks, the answer should state which number is always the same for isotopes of the same element, and which number is different. *This answer is awarded 0 out of 2 marks.*
ii $^{13}_{7}C$	The student's response is incorrect. A carbon atom cannot have proton number 7. *This answer is awarded 0 out of 1 mark.*

2 Now that you've gone through the commentary, try to write an improved answer to the parts of Question 1 where you lost marks.. This will help you check if you've understood why each mark has (or has not) been allocated. Use the commentary to guide you as you answer.

The following question has an example student commentary and answer provided. Work through the question first, then compare your answer to the sample answer and commentary. How different were your answers to the example student answers? Are there any areas where you feel you need to improve your understanding?

3 a Carbon-14 is a radioactive element.

Describe what is meant by the term *radioactive*. [2]

b The radioactive decay curve for carbon-14 is shown in Figure 3.1.

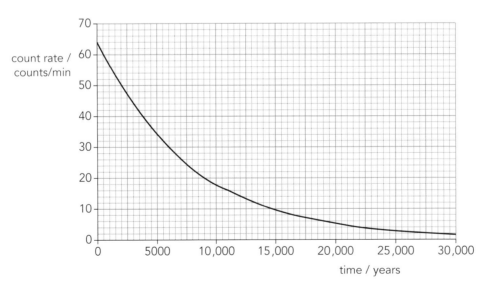

Figure 3.1

i   Complete the table using information from Figure 12.1.
     The first value has been done for you.

count rate / counts/min	time / years
40	3800
20	
10	

[1]

ii   Determine, in years, the half-life of carbon-14.   [1]

c   A radioactive iodine isotope has a half-life of 8 days.
     A sample contains 10g of this iodine isotope.

     Calculate, in g, the mass of the iodine isotope remaining in the sample
     after 16 days.   [2]

d   State **one** safety precaution taken by people who use radioactive sources.   [1]

[Total: 7]

Adapted from *Cambridge IGCSE Physics (0625) Paper 32, Q12, November 2016*

Example student response	Commentary
3 a It undergoes radioactive decay, emitting radioactivity.	The student's response is a correct statement but does not say enough about what 'radioactive' actually means. To gain 2 marks, it should mention that carbon-14 is made of atoms that are unstable, and give more detail about the decay (mentioning either that it is random or that it is spontaneous). *This answer is awarded 0 out of 2 marks.*
b i 9000 (at count rate 20) 14 000 (at count rate 10)	The first number is correct, but the second number is not. (At count rate 10, the time is one square to the left of 15 000 years. On the x-axis scale, two small squares represent 100 years, so the reading should be 14 500 years.) Both numbers need to be correct to gain the mark. *This answer is awarded 0 out of 1 mark.*
ii The half-life is the time taken for the count rate to halve. The count rate halves from 40 to 20 in a time of 9000 − 3800 = 5200 years, so the half-life is 5200 years.	The student's response is correct (but much longer than necessary – just '5200 years' would be enough to gain the mark). *This answer is awarded 1 out of 1 mark.*
c 16 ÷ 8 = 2 10 ÷ 2 = 5 g	The student has shown that they understand that 16 days equals two half-lives. However, the mass remaining is not found by dividing by the number of half-lives, but by halving for each half-life that passes. Therefore the initial amount halves twice: 10 ÷ 2 ÷ 2 = 2.5 g. *This answer is awarded 1 out of 2 marks.*
d They should handle it using long tongs.	The student's response is correct. (There are many other possible answers, including; wear a lead apron; store in a lead-lined container; and minimise the exposure time.) *This answer is awarded 1 out of 1 mark.*

Now you have read the commentary to the previous question, here is a question on a similar topic which you should attempt. Use the information from the previous response and commentary to guide you as you answer. Note, only attempt the question if you are studying for the Extended paper.

4 The radioactive isotope bismuth-210 ($^{210}_{83}$Bi) decays by β-particle emission to an isotope of polonium (Po).

    a Complete the nuclide equation that represents this decay:

$$^{210}_{83}\text{Bi} \longrightarrow {}^{\dots}_{\dots}\text{Po} + {}^{\dots}_{\dots}\beta$$
                                                    [3]

    b A radiation detector is placed on a bench in a laboratory where there are no artificial sources of radiation. The detector is switched on.

    In seven one-minute periods, the detector displays these readings.

        24   22   25   25   21   20   24

      i Explain why, in the absence of any artificial source, there are readings on the detector. Suggest **one** origin of this effect. [2]

      ii Explain why the readings obtained are not all the same. [1]

      iii The half-life of bismuth-210 is 5.0 days.

      A sample of bismuth-210 is brought close to the detector and in one minute, the reading displayed is 487. The equipment is left in the same place for exactly 10 days.

      Predict the reading in a one-minute period at the end of this time. [3]

                          [Total: 9]

Cambridge IGCSE Physics (0625) Paper 42, Q11, November 2017

The following question has an example student commentary and answer provided. Work through the question first, then compare your answer to the sample answer and commentary. Are your answers different to the sample responses? What information does this give you about your understanding of this topic?

5 Halley's Comet has been observed in the sky for over two thousand years, appearing in ancient records from Babylon and China. It is visible from Earth without a telescope for a few months every 75–79 years.

    a The volume of Halley's Comet is approximately 4×10^{11} m³ and its mass is approximately 2×10^{14} kg.

    Calculate the density of the comet, and use your result to comment on the idea that comets are largely made of ice. (The density of frozen water is 920 kg/m³.) [3]

    b Suggest why Halley's Comet is only visible in the sky for a short time within each of its orbits around the Sun. [1]

    c At its closest to Earth in 1986, Halley's Comet was at a distance of 6.3×10^7 km. Calculate the time taken for light from the comet to reach Earth when the comet was at this position. [3]

    d Explain, using the idea of conservation of energy, why a comet travels faster when it is closer to the Sun. [2]

Author-written question   **[Total: 9]**

Example student response	Commentary
5 a $\dfrac{4 \times 10^{11}}{2 \times 10^{14}} = 0.002 \, \text{kg/m}^3$ Much less dense than frozen water – the comet cannot be made of it.	The student has divided the volume by the mass. However, density = mass ÷ volume (which equals $500 \, \text{kg/m}^3$, which is consistent with the comet being made largely of ice, in addition to dust and gas). The answer is not awarded a mark for a correct formula or a mark for a correct result. However, the student has correctly deduced, based on their own calculation, that ice cannot make up a large amount of the comet, and this earns 1 mark. *This answer is awarded 1 out of 3 marks.*
b Its orbit is an ellipse so it is much further from the Sun at some times than others. We can see it when it is closer to the Sun.	The answer is correct, although longer than it needs to be to gain the mark. *This answer is awarded 1 out of 1 mark.*
c Speed of light = 3×10^5 m/s $t = \dfrac{d}{s} = \dfrac{6.3 \times 10^5}{3 \times 10^5} = 210$ s or 3.5 minutes	The student's final answer is correct, but has been reached by making two errors that have cancelled out: incorrectly recalling the speed of light, which is actually 3×10^8 m/s; and failing to convert the distance into metres (which is 6.3×10^{10} m). Therefore the student's response does not gain full marks. However, they have shown the correct equation. *This answer is awarded 1 out of 3 marks.*
d It has more energy when it is closer to the Sun, so it travels faster.	This response is incorrect. Conservation of energy means that the comet has the same energy at all points in its orbit. When it is closer to the Sun, it has less gravitational potential energy and therefore more kinetic energy, and so it has a higher speed. *This answer is awarded 0 out of 2 marks.*

Now you have read the commentary to the previous question, here is a question on a similar topic which you should attempt. Use the information from the previous response and commentary to guide you as you answer.

6   Figure 6.1 shows the Earth orbiting the Sun in an anticlockwise direction. In these images of Earth, the northern hemisphere is above the southern hemisphere.

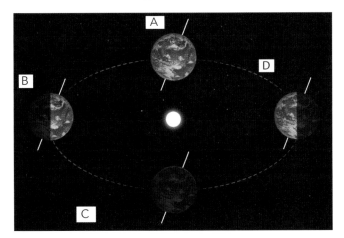

Figure 6.1

a State the season:

   i in the northern hemisphere when the Earth is at position A   [1]

   ii in the southern hemisphere when the Earth is at position B   [1]

   iii in the southern hemisphere when the Earth is at position D.   [1]

b The planet Venus takes 243 Earth days to rotate on its axis once. It takes 225 Earth days to orbit the Sun once.

   Compare the lengths of Venus's day to the length of Venus's year.   [1]

c Figure 6.2 shows the planet Uranus at four different positions, A, B, C and D, in its orbit around the Sun.

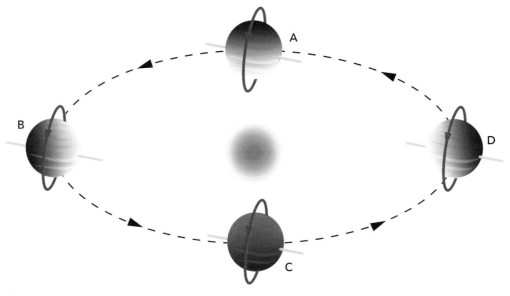

Figure 6.2

Uranus rotates about an axis shown by the straight line drawn through the planet.

Uranus 'rolls' around the Sun, and is the only planet in the Solar System that does this. It takes 17 Earth hours to rotate on its axis once, and 84 Earth years to orbit the Sun once.

   i State how much time passes between Uranus being at position A and at position C.   [1]

   ii Give the letters of the positions in the diagram at which most of the planet experiences 8.5 hours of sunlight followed by 8.5 hours of darkness.   [1]

   iii Explain why each hemisphere of Uranus experiences darkness all through its winter.   [1]

[Total: 7]

Author-written question

The following question has an example student commentary and answer provided. Work through the question first, then compare your answer to the sample answer and commentary. Where were your answers different to the sample answers?

7 **a** When a star explodes in a supernova, its remains may form a neutron star. A neutron star is made of neutrons packed closely together. Compare the density of a neutron star with the density of normal matter, and justify your response. [2]

b A supernova produces many different elements.

i State the type of reaction that forms new elements in stars. [1]

ii Explain why the Sun will never experience a supernova. [1]

Scientists have made measurements of the brightness of supernovae in the Milky Way. The distances to these can be measured.

c **i** Explain how these measurements can be used to deduce the distances to another galaxy. [2]

ii Describe a method for measuring the speed at which a galaxy is moving away from Earth. [2]

[Total: 8]

Author-written question

Example student response	Commentary
7 **a** It's much denser than normal matter, because neutrons are very dense.	The first part of the student's response is correct. The second part is not incorrect but it is not specific enough to gain the mark. More detail is needed – either: in normal matter, atoms consist mainly of empty space (whereas neutron stars do not), or: neutrons are much denser than atoms. *This answer is awarded 1 out of 2 marks.*
b **i** nuclear reaction	The reaction is a nuclear reaction but to gain the mark, the student needs to choose correctly between nuclear fusion and nuclear fission. The correct answer is nuclear fusion. *This answer is awarded 0 out of 1 mark.*
ii doesn't have enough mass	The student's response is correct. *This answer is awarded 1 out of 1 mark.*
c Observe a supernova in the other galaxy. Compare its brightness with the ones observed in our galaxy.	The student's response is correct. *This answer is awarded 2 out of 2 marks.*

Now you have read the commentary to the previous question, here is a similar question which you should attempt. Use the information from the previous response and commentary to guide you as you answer.

8

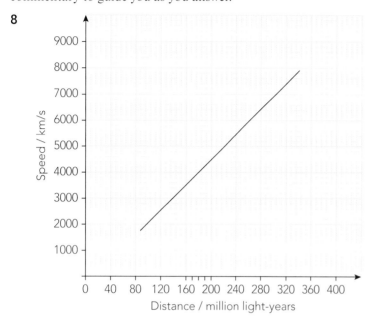

The graph shows the speeds at which galaxies are moving away from Earth, in km/s, plotted against their distance from Earth in millions of light-years. (This a best-fit line based on observations of many galaxies.)

a   Observations show that most galaxies are moving away from Earth. Explain why this does **not** mean that the Earth is at the centre of the Universe.   [1]

b   Describe the relationship that the graph shows between the speed of galaxies and their distance from Earth.   [2]

c   Calculate the number of kilometres in 1 million light-years.   [2]

d   Use the graph to calculate a value for the Hubble constant, with unit 'per second'. (For the Hubble constant to have this unit, the calculation must use distance in km.)   [3]

e   Determine the age of the Universe, using the value of the Hubble constant calculated in part **a**.   [2]

[Total: 10]

Author-written question

> Acknowledgements

The authors and publishers acknowledge the following sources of copyright material and are grateful for the permissions granted. While every effort has been made, it has not always been possible to identify the sources of all the material used, or to trace all copyright holders. If any omissions are brought to our notice, we will be happy to include the appropriate acknowledgements on reprinting.

Cambridge International copyright material in this publication is reproduced under licence and remains the intellectual property of Cambridge Assessment International Education.

Cambridge Assessment International Education bears no responsibility for the example answers to questions taken from its past question papers which are contained in this publication.

Thanks to the following for permission to reproduce images:

Cover Scotspencer/Getty Images; *Inside* Unit 1 ivanmollov/GI; Unit 3 Kolonko/GI; Unit 4 exdez/GI; Unit 5 Dirtydog_Creative/GI; Unit 9 SCIENCE PHOTO LIBRARY; Unit 16 haryigit/GI; Unit 17 JENS SCHLUETER/DDP/AFP via Getty Images; Unit 18 TREVOR CLIFFORD PHOTOGRAPHY / SCIENCE PHOTO LIBRARY, ANDREW LAMBERT PHOTOGRAPHY / SCIENCE PHOTO LIBRARY, TREVOR CLIFFORD PHOTOGRAPHY / SCIENCE PHOTO LIBRARY; Unit 24 Dorling Kindersley/GI, saemilee/GI, pijama61/GI; Unit 25 MARK GARLICK/SCIENCE PHOTO LIBRARY/GI; Exam Practice 6 Photon Illustration/Stocktrek Images/GI

GI = Getty Images

We acknowledge Amanda George as the author of chapters 1 to 11 and Exam practice 1 and 2, and Kavita Sanghvi as the author of chapters 12 to 25 and Exam practice 3 to 5.